Imperial Vistas Family Fictions

Imperial Vistas Family Fictions

KENDRICK SMITHYMAN

AUCKLAND UNIVERSITY PRESS

First published 2002

Auckland University Press
University of Auckland
Private Bag 92019
Auckland
New Zealand
http://www.auckland.ac.nz/aup

ISBN 1 86940 274 X

Publication is assisted by

Cover design by Christine Hansen

Printed by Publishing Press Limited, Auckland

Contents

List of illustrations

Introduction

According to my father, the Smithymans were originally Kendricks, of Rowton, a hamlet northwest of Wellington, or Roughton, another hamlet, three miles or so east of Bridgnorth. In either case, Shropshire. Roughton is the likelier, for continuing along the road from Bridgnorth, the A454, you are shortly brought to Wolverhampton, with which there is a family association in the nineteenth century.

Again, according to my father, a family tradition maintained the Kendrick as part of the naming although plainly not all the Smithymans were Kendrick-Smithyman with or without hyphen. His story was that the Kendricks became Smithymans in the seventeenth century, in the Restoration when a Kendrick was at or about Charles II's court. It happened when the King and a band of genial fellows were riding, and the King's horse cast a shoe. In the conjecturally less than sober buzzing about what had happened, what was going on, as part of the toing and froing, Kendrick fell off his horse and ended up clutching the leg of the King's beast, which the Merry Monarch turned into jest, of the 'Henceforth, Kendrick, you shall be my Smithyman' sort. Certainly, a Kendrick family was established in London about the time, established possibly well enough to be in the neighbourhood of Charles, but the only one of them known to me seems unlikely, a Kendrick who was an alderman and recorded by John Evelyn as a fanatic Lord Mayor.

That one part of the family did nothing to maintain the Kendrick association has to be concluded from the Smithymans, whom my father regarded as cousins, the matriarch of whom was spoken of as Aunt,

1

which actually she can scarcely have been. Father had some story of her being widowed and then forced to quit Makogai after the annexation of Fiji, a vague tale coloured by cannibals as neighbours, hurricanes, death by storm and suchlike. What is more discoverable is that Alice Smithyman, later Cooper, was born in Fiji in 1860. She was the sister of Frederick Charles Smithyman, who was born at Rewa, Fiji, in 1863, said to be the first white male born in the group. He was the eldest son of John Bailey Smithyman, who was a merchant of Wolverhampton but migrated, to plant cotton in the boom years coinciding with the American Civil War, although I do not know what he did otherwise apart from marry the daughter of 'a late Major Merrill of the Imperial army'. What relation was he to my grandfather? I cannot say. Father seemed to think of Frederick Charles as his uncle, which is quite wrong. He regarded Alice Cooper as his cousin, so inferentially John Bailey was an uncle and as such my grandfather's brother. Frederick Charles's son, William Frederick, who was of an age with Father – they first met on a soccer field in Auckland when a call for Bill Smithyman produced two youngsters to discover their kinship – was a cousin but at a further step removed. They met amiably in years after but seldom sought a meeting. I went to the 'Aunt's' funeral; I think I was taken once to visit her at her home. Father had little impulse to keep his kinship there warm. Indeed, he spoke little about his father's family. What did my great-grandfather Smithyman do? I have no idea. I assume, it is only assumption, he was named William Kendrick and maybe he was, since some kind of insistence appears to have derived from my grandfather, but what were my great-grandmother Smithyman's names? I've no idea.

Grandfather Smithyman went to sea. Born in 1829, he served in the Royal Navy during the Crimean War, having both the Crimea medal (with the Sebastapol clasp) and the Baltic medal. To that extent he was a Navy man. From something once said in passing, I gathered the Navy had been his career in his early years, but he must have taken his discharge not long after the war, because he was on the goldfields of Victoria as a warden in the heyday of those fields. When he left them, he sailed for England with some notion of returning to Australia, for he had bought a piece of land in Melbourne. Whatever plans he had were sharply arrested. His ship was wrecked on the coast of Patagonia. He had no companions. He was taken by Indians at a time when the Argentinians were clearing lands of any and all Indians, who were moving south and were not inclined to let

Grandfather go north or to have any contact with Europeans. During the next three or four years Grandfather shifted further and further south, finally reaching the Straits of Magellan. He stole a canoe and crossed to Tierra del Fuego, working his way along the shore until, as spring passed into summer he accumulated a food supply and, rounding the tip at Cape San Diego, made a desperate gamble. He put out to sea, vaguely but implausibly 'south of the Horn', hoping to meet with a ship homeward bound from Australia or New Zealand . . . and obviously did so.

Another blank, and another inference. He married, and he and Grandmother went out to Calcutta, probably to the Hooghly River pilotage. This is inferred, from a suggestion once made that if Father did not want to go on in the Merchant Service he might think of becoming a Hooghly River pilot, and from a reported saying of Grandfather: 'Man that is born of a woman has but a short time. He goes up like a rocket and he comes down like a bloody Bromley kite', which is a notable carrion bird of the Hooghly. Slim evidence, but another fragment points to that part of the world, Father saying of his younger brother Arthur: 'Sticks was so small when he was born the ayah used to bath him in a quart pot.' Father had been years dead before it occurred to me what was implied here, and along with it a far recollection of something said about 'the ayah' connected with Gloucester, no more than that. An excursion to Calcutta, the pilotage, an ayah brought back to England. That's all there is.

Grandfather Smithyman was almost fifty when Father was born. Since there was no obvious wide range to cover the births of his children he must have been in his forties when he married. Grandmother Smithyman outlived him by more than thirty years, and was eightyish at her death whereas he (who died before he was seventy), had he lived, would have been pressing on a hundred. If twenty years younger, Grandmother was born around 1850, which puts her main childbearing into her twenties, which seems reasonable.

Returned to England, Grandfather established a home at Westbury-on-Severn (at Stantway House) and a business as a wine and spirit merchant, more likely in Gloucester city. Traffic on the river was no light matter. Westbury itself is not on the river, but not far off (less than half the distance for travelling than commuting to Gloucester would require) is Newnham-on-Severn, a riverside and cargo-handling village in those days, so his business may have been there. It was at Newnham that Father, if no other of the family, was christened. If you carry on from Newnham on the once Roman road to Chepstow, you will pass through Lydney, where not long before Father was born Grandfather and

Grandmother Evans were getting ready to migrate to New Zealand with their then two children.

At Westbury, whatever the requirements of his business Grandfather Smithyman rode to hounds and was a wholehearted Freemason. While hunting he took a toss and broke his legs. This did not stop him from insisting on attending, however awkwardly, a meeting of his lodge that night. Borne on a stretcher he made it, and entered indeed wholeheartedly into the procedure of the lodge to the point of forgetfulness, the point at which the service called for him to rise to his feet which he tried to do. This, it was said, was the only time Grandfather ever fainted. Father was at times a Mason and should have known what he was talking about, but was also at times likely to gild his story, so I have no way of knowing how true it was that Grandfather advanced to whatever degree in Masonry and might be called upon to serve as standard bearer to the Prince of Wales in his lodge duties, even accompanying Wales to France on occasion. We touch the hem of the gown. It will be seen later we touch that hem otherwise.

Grandfather did not stay with the wine and spirits. He moved his family to Ramsgate where he was to be harbourmaster. The boys went to a preparatory school of some moderate reputation, Chatham House, with boys from India and boys from France of families in a network of wine dealings who were Protestants as well.

The harbourmastering cannot have been too onerous. One daily duty was observed, required by Grandmother who was pious, and the harbour took second place to that. Grandfather had to read a chapter of the Bible. This he did in the conservatory, walking to and fro, '. . . these are the names of the men *sweet sweet sweet* that shall stand with you *sweet*; of the tribe of Reuben *sweet boy there's a boy*' mixed with suitable little whistlings to his birds. The house had a conservatory, and accommodated the two girls of the family who were apparently day girls at a no doubt genteel school not far off, the three boys who were boarders at Chatham House, Grandmother and Grandfather, a cook-housekeeper, a maid? In later years Grandmother lived with Agnes, Arthur, and the housekeeper Mrs Steele, who remained after Grandmother and Agnes were dead, caring for Arthur into the Second World War until Arthur was evacuated to Tunbridge Wells. The later years were at 9 Vale Square, which as I remember from a photograph could not readily have made space enough for all the family, plus domestics, let alone run to a conservatory and which, when I saw the house, was even smaller, having been rebuilt after wartime damage. So I have no picture of the house which became the

5

6

family home after they left Gloucester, only the vignette of Grandfather walking – Father was emphatic about that – up and down as he read his chapter, or sitting, glass beside glass with his younger kinsman Pelham Aldrich in that conservatory, taking a tot, reminiscing (we can be sure about that) and gossiping (Pelham was convinced the Duke of York morganatically married Elsie Tryon, and Pelham because of his position at the Malta station was in a better position than most to know such things).

Pelham survives in a small way as a watercolourist, by virtue of the watercolours he made while serving on *Challenger* on that great voyage of exploration of the 1870s, but more by his journal which his sketches illustrated. He was summoned to leave for other exploring, from which came his Arctic Medal. His name occurs in the society novels of A Gentleman with a Duster, who mentions him along with, say, Mrs Cornwallis-West. He had more to him than that; he was, like Elsie Tryon's unfortunate father, a most professional long-serving naval officer who commanded at Portsmouth and at Malta and sat to drink with Grandfather Smithyman, to whom he was rather junior, a contemporary more of Grandmother.

Among the kin of whom Pelham Aldrich was one were two men of law, one tall, one not so, known as The Long and The Short of the Law. The name of The Long fellow escapes me. He had two daughters and a passion for tennis, was said to be among the first in England to lay down a hard court. He had two daughters and no anxiety to get them off his hands, for they were useful in making a foursome and even more so in providing him with an opponent when no one outside the family was available; for instance, in winter, when the girls might be, indeed were, sent out to clear snow from the court (as Father remembered) to allow for practice, which was no doubt considered good for them. No such formidable story attached to The Short, who comes down as Uncle Wotton, who was Something-or-other Wotton-Isaacson, of a Cornish family with mining interests, even an iron-master or two, although whatever I hear of Uncle Wotton suggested nothing of the hardheaded thrusting Victorian industrialist.

The Long and The Short presumably had chambers handy for meeting to proceed amiably to lunch each working day without debate as to where that lunch would be, for Simpson's in the Strand entirely suited them, although one may think there must have been times when Wotton's responsibilities at the Inner Temple would have demanded him. It was to Simpson's as Father grew that Wotton took him, as he did his son Egerton. Father was fond of both father and son, they continued warmly

7

remembered. The Long man was respected, admired, he cut a figure and a dash without any of the brashness, one feels it was how they were regarded, of F. E. Smith or Marshall Hall. The Short man was enduringly a figure not of dash but simple affection who certainly commanded respect among his colleagues. He died as Warden of the Inner Temple. The obituary tributes in the press were not many or extensive but Uncle Wotton's quality was made clear.

At some time in my boyhood I realised that Nana Campbell was not my grandmother but who was my mother's mother was not made clear. Nor, consequently, although I knew she was Annie Lavinia, did I get to know my mother's maiden name. Since she was not a churchgoing woman I failed to identify her with Annie Evans who on Christmas Day 1911 wrote her name in the Prayer Book (bound in red leather, one cover a pocket like a purse for the offering or as my prosaic Mum said, for tram or bus tickets) which survives although only barely. It was not worn out by devotion.

   My mother talked about the Campbells when she talked about family. Eventually I believed they were to all intents and purposes her family, they fostered her as they would another and younger girl, and they took her in to help Nana with her children. About her schooling I can't remember her saying anything, where she was when she went to school, or when she quit school, which I imagine she did at thirteen, a common leaving age and one that would suit quite well for a household aid. If there was not a considerable gap between her age and Nana's, as I think was the case, then the fostering was not in the first instance by Campbells but by Nana's birth-family, who in due season passed her on. My impression is that she lived at Nana Campbell's long after she stopped being a baby minder. When, in short, she went to work outside the home, that home (for so long 481 Manchester Street, St Albans, Christchurch) was surely the matriarch's rather than the domain of any patriarchal figure. Alec Campbell was a Lyttelton watersider (I think I'm right about that) who was physically larger than Nana, slower moving, less volatile. I recall a white shirt and a dark waistcoat going thoughtfully down his garden path with his friend Jack, his pet magpie, to find Jack some worms.

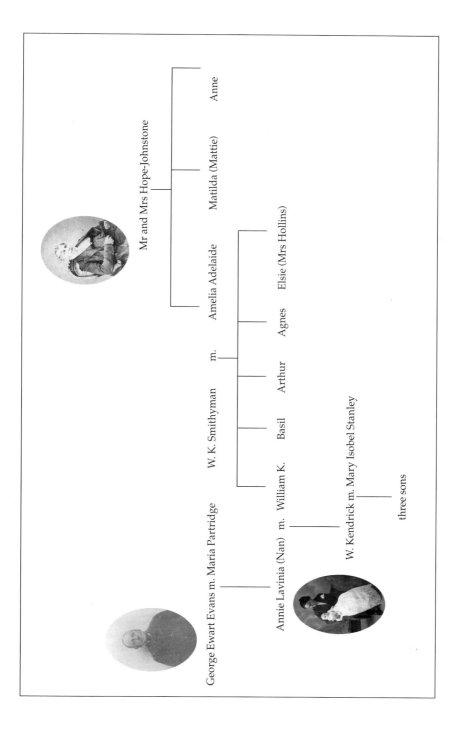

Mr and Mrs Hope-Johnstone

George Ewart Evans m. Maria Partridge   W. K. Smithyman   m.   Amelia Adelaide   Matilda (Mattie)   Anne

Annie Lavinia (Nan) m. William K.   Basil   Arthur   Agnes   Elsie (Mrs Hollins)

W. Kendrick m. Mary Isobel Stanley

three sons

Wild Goats

Back from the regatta at Pahi
gimpy Father drunk as a skunk clambered
broad steps of the Home, waved to who
ever drove the Rugby for him, addressed
Mother: "If I had ten thousand a year
I'd be damned if I employed a chauffeur.
I'd drive my own car. Madam, where is
the taproom?" "Why, sir, in here,"
and locked him in the bathroom.
He'd probably been drinking with Gordon Coates.
Gordon was about to be Prime Minister,
Father was busy with the local Labour branch.

They did not know how to conduct themselves.
They were unpardonable. They had style.

In a season of riots he borrowed ten bob
to call on the Duchess of Perlmutter
at the Grand. "Shelagh's in town," he told us
who were remotely of his kind.
"I should really go to see her," and did.
                                    And, of Starkie
who hearing Gordon was up from Wellington
left them in the backbar of the Auckland,
went up to the Grand, pushed into the dining
room, hit up Gordon for a fiver: "I said to him,
Gordon, the day I bought you back out of No
Man's Land was the best day's work I did
for me, the worst I ever did for this poor
bloody misgoverned country." No
man's land. What do we do? What do we
do?
    It isn't true, all men are brothers.
Father did not care for Shelagh's brother
whom he called Georgey. He did not care for
Winston's brother Jack.

11

The other day Jed took
his pack, roll, thirty-thirty and young dog
Mac. He headed for the tops where it cost
regulated forestry fifty thousand to shoot
out the wild goats. It's all regenerating.
He couldn't find any of the tracks.
He had a rough time.

an arrow one shade more to right or left

Grandfather bound for home (with, there'd have
to be, Australian gold) rounds the Horn,
ends up on the Patagonia coast said to be
rather like Caledonia stern and wild.
Did anyone else survive? He didn't know.
He started tramping to the Plate.

Indians wouldn't let him. They were going south.
He went south, handed from tribe to tribe.
Finally, Magellan's Strait, he made his break,
stole a canoe, crossed over, trapped, dried fish.
He worked his way round the Land of Fires.
The end of all America is rocky, crossgrained.
Bleak, it goes against nurture.

Grandfather kitted himself out between islands.
Perhaps he prayed for a few days' fine weather.
Fine weather came. He put out to sea,
paddling
          for the Horn, for beyond, reckoned
a ship might happen by from (maybe) New Zealand,
California, Valparaiso – he was right.
Summer was signing off three years late.

                    * * *

He didn't talk about this, unless to Pelham.
Pelham was once in those parts, not with *Challenger*
as you'd expect.
                    Grandmother didn't know;
she asked him to read each day a chapter,
to give thanks. He walked up/down up/down
in a hothouse with an aviary. 'Now these are
the generations of the sons of Noah
sweet sweet sweet Shem, Ham, and Jappheth:
and unto them were *sweet!* were sons born
after the flood.' He liked names, they were
consoling. He liked Jonah too.

The family heard, only by accident.

13

Summer of '82

Travel broadens outlooks.
His aunts took Willy abroad – naturally, Paris,
provincial Germany, the Festspielhaus? Munich,
Vienna, Venice, the Acropolis,
home by way of Malta. Corfu was best:
        Easter, the Orthodox paraded streets,
processed St Spyridion embalmed, triggered
shotguns joyfully bawling "Christ is risen!"
bang then *bang* again. Pantocrator delirious
flew strips of cloud, Albanian mountains glowered.
Christ is risen. Around the Esplanade bands played,
not very well. Visitors were told, at such times
voices were heard to wail along dry shores
        Great Pan is dead.
All too soon they'd be sailing Home.

Malta: bustling angry beards bristled for action
against Arabi and Alex. The French, too,
going to be difficult, would sail home leaving
Beauchamp Seymour
                        giving Alexandrians notice
how his intentions were plain, if criminal.
O Isis und Osiris, great Pan was dead indeed.

What flute at nightfall mourned imperial
magic, which Armstrong guns should not excel?
Quickfiring summer stormed walls low,
in Corfu halfpay colonels looked to laurels,
with their sidearms. St Michael and St George,
the Widow, Billy Gladstone, Sir Garnet,
Evelyn Wood, they stood to arms. Came the four
corners almost of the world to Arabi,
saints, sirdars and society, a gorgeous
pandemonium.
                Willy remembered most
Greek shotguns blaring Christ! Oh Christ is risen!
Turkish delight, a Corfiote puppet play.

Educating Father

Chatham House, a prep school: distinguished
Indians, some I.C.S. and Anglos helpful at
cricket, and (mainly coastal) French boys,
the wine trade. It all helped.
Grandmother's Anglican connections,
they might also help along with the family French
which crossed over into Québec.
Modus vivendi, a phrase one had to learn.
After harbourmastering Grandfather merchant
        went into wines and spirits.

        Precocious in contract,
Father arrived at modes of survival,
came to an understanding with his Head –
for dodging classes, a measure of tolerance
figured against a catch of fish.
Much depended on fishermen's connivance
who concurred until

                an uncle who built
railways this way and that in the Americas
(built in Argentina, built in Canada)
sent a birthday present, a birchbark canoe.
Fishermen helped rig a sail.

Willy set out, was picked up after panic
between Calais and Boulogne. The canoe
passed to a museum, Willy – "Not the Navy,"
his mother insisted, and had her way –
Willy they packed off to *Worcester*,
the merchant navy for him.

17

Marking Man

Worcester: At fourteen or so Father was
found in the netting under the bowsprit
with the Captain's daughter. Her Papa thought
the lad ready for sea. From that time
Father was a marked man
                              a tattoo on his left arm
Devitt and Moore, his first apprenticeship.
They went out of business. Right forearm,
Shaw Savill and Albion. New Zealand was forecast.
The Shaws were also said to be kin.
It's not clear how this may have been helpful.

Pelham

liked watercolouring, given
a glass or two with Grandfather liked
gossiping. Pelham himself, well now,
he was a chap put into the knowledgeably
hinting novels of A Gentleman with a Duster,
along with folk like Mrs Cornwallis-West
or the Jersey Lily, in settings like
the Malta station. He was marriage kin,
goodlooking with it. In the know
how far
as they sat (in the conservatory?)
heads credibly/informedly together,
rings of glasses on their ironwork table
briefly locking, interlocking, then wiped
away.
Clarence predictably, we all know
what was said about Clarence sub rosa and sotto;
but Clarence died in his delirium at Sandringham
of which are only hints of harrowing,
only hints of. Left his fiancée, May

who was taken over by brother York,
they married

and *Victoria* rammed by *Camperdown* sank
off the lesser Tripoli under command of
Admiral Tryon who had if not brilliant then start
lingly competent career behind him. "Why,"
says P. reportedly,
"because the poor fellow was
out of his mind   because York was marrying
that German gel, May, Teck's (and he's crazy)
daughter
while morganatically married
to Elsie Tryon"
and they wiped away no doubt
and interlocking rings. *Sweet sweet sweet* sang
Grandfather's birds in their various cages.

Knitting

Things one didn't get the hang of,
like,
　　　until the other day checking
Who was Who, how Pelham fitted in.
Not just a friend or someone from
Navy days, he was/must have been
brother-in-law to (Great) Uncle
Wotton who
　　　short, quiet, bookish,
did not receive the Arctic Medal
or more notable decorations
Pelham had.
　　　Respecting law,
became Warden of the Inner Temple.
Father always spoke of him fondly,
was deeply fond of Wotton's son,
Cousin Egerton, who joined the Service.

　　　When Pelham commanded
at Portsmouth Egerton was posted
overseas. He enjoyed a night out
(Cape Town) with Father, missed
his ship, caught up at Durban,
and lost three years' seniority.
Contemptus mundi does not pay.

Twenty and a bit years later
Egerton, due for the New Zealand
station, dock superintendent
Portsmouth, was called out to
some emergency at the base,
rushed down in his sporty Sunbeam
tourer, and on to an oil spill.
Populace and priest alike shall be
　　　forgot.
He left no wife, no children,
O Atropos, mistress
　　　of the forgetful shades of night

Whatever Became

North bound a night train hauls from some
piddling point in a nowhere darkness,
a traveller settling back happens to glance out
where a face tilts momently into detail
at the waitingroom doorway – could that
have been? No need to enlarge on this,
we all know how

> *quite alone*
> *to me there came a fellow I have known*
> *in some old times*

Father chatting about Ramsgate caused
a face to look back. "People used to move
from London for the summer, it was easy
for the men to travel up and down.
Next to us or somewhere near us anyway,
family of a judge, Vaughan Williamses.
Mother was friendly with, probably
because of her uncle, Judge Holland.
They had a son, a nephew? biggish quiet chap.
I've quite forgotten his name. Sticks would be
bound to know. They were musical."

Sundown, shadows in the Square.
Across, boys looked at boys, briefly. Turned away.

Uncle Arthur

His brothers named him Sticks,
he was spindly. "He was so small when he was born,
the ayah used to say, she could bath him
in a quart pot." He had two enthusiasms,
cricket and church organs. As a boy
he was one of those who bowled W. G.

Arthur never went to work except at
houseparties, cricketing, churchcrawling.
He survived on a dwindling matrimony,
Grandmother's legacy from Judge Holland
invested in Argentine railways
by whatever uncle built miles of them.
Father was no hand at investments
or letter writing; at six or seven I had
to take over, *Dear Uncle Arthur I am starting
to collect stamps* to which a postscript,
"Dear Sticks, I am well. How are you? Can you
let me have fifty quid?"

Twice Uncle Arthur bettered random
advances made by Germans. He was somehow
bombed out, I suppose he was what you'd call
a decayed gentleman when he passed
at Tunbridge Wells in the Attlee era,
caught and bowled in the midcentury
of the Common Man. His last housekeeper
was desolate.

Another

(great) uncle whose name
I can't recover,
also of the Temple?
Very tall, sedate,
a dedicated man,
he and Wotton
lunched together
at Simpson's.
One squat, one lofty,
"They were known as
the Long and Short
of Law". His passion
was tennis, he was among
the first who laid down
a hard court in England.
In winter he drove
his matchless girls
out to (if need be)
sweep snow from the court.
If they couldn't net
anyone else, they could
at least play singles,
or, as to duty bound,
they could partner him.

Great Aunt Anne

Great Aunt Anne   eighty years older
than me, had no children. Her husband
a tea merchant, they lived at Maidenhead.
Was it said she had been in waiting?
To whom?   It did not concern that
at eighty-eight she would write a neat
small hand to my mother, to send
an embroidery pincushion truly like
a cushion, hand sewn with neatest gold
thread stitches. Saying
"I wish you to have this. I shall not be
any longer able to sew. My physician tells me
any time now I must think of needing
spectacles." Her younger sister, Mattie,
was long since blind. Mattie had no children.

High Romance

The High Romantic, its bleak affluent face.

Somewhere along the line a French connection
with the du Plessis, legacy of exile
from '30 or '48. By way of this
one of the girls proposed to marriage
into France was crossed to Paris,
to somewhere further, provincial,
waited her man returning from the wars.

Dim sounds of horsemen and parade,
pale air of fête, people climbed to rooftops,
streets lined, she at a window, he looks up,
perhaps he waves . . . a tile dislodged
took him right out of the saddle as she watched
her sequel to Sedan?
                        The story's faded
like many of the prints, may still display
squalid in some unimportant corner
the High Romantic's affronted deathly face.

Rounding the Horn

Father never grew tall.
Grandmother put it down to his third voyage:
Forfarshire making the Horn was swept and pooped.
Everything aloft went over the side,
seas grabbed chronometers out of the chartroom.
From then on they worked four on—four off,
in their four off they stood two hours at the pumps.
Jury-rigged they took six weeks to round the Horn.
Captain James was one of the few who preferred
usually to go through the Straits. That voyage
he chose wrong.
           The Captain had his pocket watch.
In the South Atlantic he met one ship
which reported them: "Spoke a hulk with some
      canvas flying, said she was *Forfarshire*."
At Lloyds the first bell had been rung.
      On the strength of his watch and that fix
James made his landfall, off Land's End,
carried on to London. Grandfather watched
from Ramsgate as they limped, refusing tugs.

"Willy," Father was asked, "would you like to join
the Hudson's Bay Company?" Between voyages
he went out; he didn't like it; he came back.
He sailed for New Zealand.
           Captain James was
killed on the wharf at Lyttelton,
a block falling as they rigged ship.

Eating

Someone in a pub:
"I saw him once in Flanders, sitting on the side of a road.
He scrounged a piece of bacon so ripe and greasy
the cook wouldn't try to palm it off on us.
But there was Bill, both hands at it – and the look
on his face, like it was a delicacy."

Father was fond of boiled bacon. Also, pickled pork,
corned beef, and muttonbirds. He learned young,
with useful hints or recipes as
How to cook a muttonbird. Place (skinned, gutted,
split) in a frying pan, cook until ready.
Will do for some other birds too, seabirds
of course.
                If you open a cask of salt beef/
salt horse and it's really black and stinking,
put the meat in a canvas bag and tow it astern
for twenty-four hours. Pound with a chipping hammer.
Take ship's biscuits especially if with weevils,
break up biscuits, throw in with meat,
boil until thick pudding-like and can be
got down. This saves picking out weevils
and makes biscuits and meat more tasty.

On *Forfarshire* the casks were date-stamped for Crimea.
Forty years in the brine, the meat beat them.
Almost beat them, the ABs sawed chunks,
air dried them, cut them down, bored them out,
carved pipe bowls from them and knick-knacks
to sell in port. This was called
Sailing Under the Red Duster.

Cutty Sark

In company with *Cutty Sark* at sea
only once, on *Himalaya* off Brazil.
They sailed into the doldrums.
Day after day another sail came into sight,
would lose the wind, then idle.
Forty-two ships counted from the masthead.

Sent up with a glass at daybreak
to mark if anything stirred, reported
a clipper coming from the south carrying
canvas, the mate observing from the poop
later was first to say *"That's Cutty Sark."*
They watched her through the day.
At last light she was hull down, northing,
had sailed right through the might as well
have been derelict fleet, forty-plus of them,
some getting on for four weeks there.

That's what poetry may be about, the impossible
part of it which achieves insubstantial
fact, as little material as Sybil Sanderson's
G in alt or Fonteyn's unpredicted change
('If you didn't see why I did it when I did
it then it didn't work') not to be described;
when seen, if seen, in kind a dumbshow
to strike dumbstruck any who looked out
hearing something beyond likely hearing,
seeing something not likely seen, gone
without leaving words for.

Bard

Masefield mentions 'sweep *Cupica*, tall *Bard*
Queen in all harbours with her moonsail yard'.
Asking him, "What's this about a moonsail yard?"
he remembers only one ship mounting a moonraker,
"The *Bard*, a tall ship, she lay across
the wharf from us at Callao. It made you dizzy
just to look aloft.
                      We all went off to the cantinas
one night, the gendarmes grabbed us and threw us
into the calaboose, boys off the *Bard*, us, chaps
from a baldheaded barque lying further along . . .
Someone set fire to the calaboose, we kicked out
the doors, beat it back to our ships.
The shippers sent for the Consul.
After that we stayed aboard.
                                    But the *Bard*,
God, she was a tall ship. You looked up,
all that gear, way up there – "

still marvellous.

Visitor

Dumpy shortsighted young man, thick
moustaches, wandering Queen Street buys
a special blend for his pipe at Coleman's.

Then a turn around the wharves – that's
Mister Kipling already something of a name if
not as yet married. Hard put to believe it,

seeing him perhaps at ease with a beer,
a barmaid. (He'd call her 'Mrs Bathurst'.)
But now he's strolling Queen's Wharf?

Will he ride the ferries? Not today,
he's trying to arrange a passage to Samoa,
he wants to visit with R.L.S. who half

expects him, but gives up. The Samoa fruit
boat skipper isn't coming off the grog
for a while. 'All I carried away from Auckland . . .

the face and voice of a woman' which he'd
hear again in Cape Town, a few memories:
how he reached the north by buggy, his driver

gone a bit queer in the head, a horse's skull
beside the track, wild horses on a nameless
plain. Somewhere along the way he was fed

roast kiwi; the skin, like pork crackling.
He did New Zealand in twelve days. Still,
he spoke with old Sir George, sailed out
    with General Booth.

Visitor Two

Where was David Balfour? He was needed,
the High Commissioner at Suva turning nasty,
talking of sedition. Ebb tide, the beach awash
at Falesa. Health was poorly.

He, Belle and Fanny sailed off brewing up
Weir the Lord-Justice Clerk, on a gadabout;
Mariposa took them in and out of Auckland.
Silk stockings for the ladies (Colvin's text
reads 'sick'), for him 'always a white shirt,
white necktie, fresh shave, silk socks,
O a great sight! No more possible'
after
walking with Sir George upon his arm,
discoursing. And Sir George approved.

He was not forthcoming to the Press
(was it Jimmy Cowan?), nor was he reported
lecturing/talking at the Northern Club.
He came. He went. Passed through
back to Samoa. Boys at the wharf saw
a sick man who wrote *Kidnapped*,
fathers of the town a man who was into
politics, casting (they could not foretell)
a long sad shadow nor
                        might hear New
Zealand gunfire clamouring against
the Mau, processional.

Viking

Close to one hundred years ago,
music and wester sunshine walking the waters:
Waitemata summer, enduring summer.

The South Seas hadn't heard of winter,
not until they shaped course for the Horn
along with
                    Jesus Christ skipjacks, storm petrel, molly
          mawk and albatross, skua, homebound arctic tern.
Holds, full of wool, kauri gum maybe.
End of season, before the weather,
                                        but in harbour

Island schooners, brigs, coastal scows, timber
rafts and their tugs, cutters, all manner
of steam craft
                    and yachts with room for
youngsters crewing in time off along
with Auckland boys, racing, cruising.
Grandfather had a cousin, how else?
At first he was Mayor with sons of his own,
he made welcome; Father was one of the boys
feathered white wings which never grew weary.
Not *I dreamt that I dwelt in marble halls*
up St Stephens or round Judges Bay, more like
The moon has raised her lamp above
Mansion House, Tryphena, Coromandel?
          with ditties suited Reserve training.
On H.M.S. *Rattle*, always summer,
gannet diving, kahawai birds danced.
They went their ways, they met, they parted

across the Vaal, before the Somme, in wardrooms,
in boardrooms some, some in Ellerslie saddling paddock,
those who succeeded, those who did not,
that was their Age of Gold.
                              The colonial
web shivered; they did not notice.

If you asked, suppose you could
ask, "Look back now" as he did look "and give me
one image most of all which catches
what was of all the best, which held in one
what fifty years of settlement arrived at
while promising, still promising, could be?"
    why, yes, he could
                        Viking
up from the Gulf under full canvas homing,
a firm nor'easter making music in the shrouds.

Unsuitable Positions

for young persons, tried between/
looked at/looked over/were mentioned,
at least one between voyages
                    Hudson's Bay Company.
The Hooghli River pilotage, of course,
the Canal in passing
        looked at, looked over, considered
points further east
mysteriously.

                    At some time he aimed for
an Old China Hand, a stopover at Shanghai,
a quick trip up the Yangtze
rather boring
                    convoying silk lighters
coming down in season. He was
a Maxim gunner just in case of
bandits or river pirates, no more
than a look upcountry?

Didn't like it, went somewhere
else, back Home, off again.

Grandfather, Life and Death

A night on the town around the Halls,
last train home to Ramsgate. "Is that you,
Willy?" who was seldom home. Grandfather,
propped on pillows, read late, married late,

  served in the Baltic squadron and at
  Sebastopol too.
In Victoria he was a goldfields warden.
Returning from, was wrecked; three years among Patagonians.
Married, he joined the Hooghli River pilotage,
picked up a saying: 'Man that is born of a woman
  hath but a short time to live. He goeth up like
  a rocket, he comes down like a Bromley kite.'
Grandmother was distressed by Calcutta.

  Hunting in Gloucester he took a toss to break
both legs, insisted on going to Lodge that night
(was he ever standard bearer to the Prince?)
but during Lodge forgot. He tried to stand.
"The only time in my life, I fainted."

When he had gout he was not patient.
His gout was his legacy, he passed it on
in a small way: of five children, only one child;
    of that child, only one child.
Grandfather asked Willy about night in London,
The White-Eyed Kaffir, Little Tich, Marie Lloyd.
It was late. He closed his book.
"Pour me my tot, please."

He finished his glass. He put his churchwarden
  on the bedtable. He folded his hands.
He said, "Well, boy, I'm for off."

Turning Tables

General Bindon Blood arrived late at the party
in the Transvaal, still in time to cut a caper.
He and his son were thought a roistering pair
around London clubland. "They called 'em
Bloody Senior and Bloody Junior."

Young Blood took something wrong in his chest.
Doctors recommended leave from his regiment,
a long sea voyage. His father felt that wouldn't
hurt at all; besides, he could profitably learn
the harbourfinding art. He was shipped apprentice,
old man of the middies' mess. He was not

much at rope work or at handling boats
yet had a flair, for navigating. Of course he knew
something already, handling sextant, pencil,
a scrap of paper. "Mister Mate, pray, what is
that young man doing?" working out a position
without tables.
                   The tables were in his head.
He found it bothersome out in the open
book in hand, winds might be a nuisance.
Easier, just to get them off. All you do
is read them over a few times, after that
you keep them in your head, you turn pages
when you need to, you read off – "It's just
a knack, sir, like being good at games" –
Nothing to it. Merely read on,
log, antilog, tan, cotan.

Imperial Vistas

Blessed may be the meek knowing they shall
not inherit their earth
                    from Grandmother,
from Grandfather, who are not in Heaven as
yet. Only, close to it, Thy Will be done will
be done
                    Father was very (was too?) small to
remember Victoria at (probably) Windsor
where his grandaddy sometimes preached.
Boys of Eton might be on hand to cheer,
the loyal townsfolk anyway you could rely
on. And trippers – you ought to be able to count
on them. The East End was always,
                                    you know,
but among them a kid about my father's size
who did not make his signal. The carriage
stopped, someone flung himself down
suitably to chastise. Respect, that's what
has to be learned. Respect. Learn early,
learn it long, your legacy.

            At Pretoria, after the Raid,
before the big shootup started
young Father was with his cobber Frikkie,
supposedly Oom Paul's favourite
grandson, a bad boy. Over the road from
the Dopper church, Mrs Kruger sold milk
to her neighbours; she was a simple frugal soul.
In a milkwhite highveld night
Father and Frikkie approached, that night of sort
with Olive Schreiner's when 'frank and unreserved
confession will obviate the necessity
of chastisement' perhaps. House people came
to the stoep. Grandfather sat
in the brilliant moonlight with his Bible,
his churchwarden pipe. Whatever
was he reading should bear on the case?

A Kaffir offended: "Take him round
the back, sjambok him," and back
to the Book. Thy Will be

                    done will be done

Vision

Something, perhaps the way his beer tasted
or tobacco smoke clouding, reminded
of many. A manly throat would creditably
tighten, an eye be moistened in the saloon,
nostalgically or covetously
at thought of
                          not that all was sentimental.
The mine manager's wife now, Mrs ——
(as oldfashioned novels used to say)
who gleamed more remote from them than any
prospected horizon, who was to be
treated like a lady, not aspired to.
They all knew her only in a manner of speaking,
how not? She drove
                          a spanking little cart fast,
a pair of zebra in the shafts, or when
fancy took her rode behind a handpicked
halfdozen Zulu in full kit, cavorting,
flashing eyes, playing to dusty
galleries' scandalised shutters.

When fancy took her she'd go round by night
in and out of places where men drank
as they gambled. "Man, once I saw her
climb on a table in the flashest of saloons
to damn them all for chickenhearted moneygrubbers.
She auctioned herself for the night
to the first who would put up
a thousand guineas"
then took her pick from all the takers.

Animal Studies

One of the Marais clan talking
           Baboons came around like they are now, squatting
up there. They stole a baby, a toddler.
Naturally it took a while to work out
where the boy had gone,
                  then everybody was off
after them but they were well away.
We, the family, hunted them for years.
Every so often another report: a pack of apes,
a human child with them. He was into
his teens before we captured him.
Brought back here
           he never learned to talk.
He didn't try to get loose. Once in a while
baboons arrived to work the district,
they'd sit up there and howl.
He howled back at them, rattled his chain.
After a few years he died. They still come
back

One of the Maritz clan
           but nobody knows
how old he is. He was fully grown before
he was taken, that was before the Trek,
as fully grown, you know, as they get to.
We think he's the last of something
older than Hottentots and Bushmen
because he isn't properly Hottentot and he is
'nt properly Bushman. No one can
talk to him – well, a few words he's learned.
When the weather is good he climbs that tree
to sleep. What he most likes is when
there's a dead beast, pull the guts out of it,
he crawls inside. He likes that,
           while it lasts,
best while it's warm and does more than
keep the wind out. After that, a few days
and nights it's good too

Perhaps not the same Marais
  also I like to watch ants.
You can learn a lot from ants.
But come along,
     bring a stick.
You don't need a rifle, just a stick.
It does as well. They don't seem to recognise
any difference. I will tell you

how the big dog controls his people?
No. How, if/when they are foraging or on
the move one of the pack falls into some crevice
and (say) breaks a leg, what they do?
These baboons are shrewd.
Oh yes, I have read Kropotkin
so I tell you

they fetch up the one that's wounded.
(This means they may have to go further and further.)
They bring clay and puddle it by pissing.
They mould the clay round the broken limb.
They keep it cool by peeing on it.
They keep it in place by holding it; in turn
they sit, holding it. Or, and, they use
(*maybe I am inventing this bit*)
banana leaves or mealie leaves, poulticing.

  This was quite a while ago. Father had to
remember, I am trying to remember what Father
was telling about a time before or after
another war, but that was in another country
and besides Marais is dead.

Perhaps the same Maritz
     Come and try
drinking our brandywine. Do you think
really there's going to be fighting?

Looking at *Picture Post*

series on the war in South Africa
when another war was shaping up

The railway station at Jo'burg,
Uitlanders getting out while there was
time: "Those fellows there, miners.
A lot of them were Cornishmen, they were
very sentimental. Get someone to sing
The Miner's Dream of Home in a hall or a bar
and they'd cry, they'd bawl, they'd pelt
the stage with money. People called them
Cousin Yacks, they couldn't say a J." –

– "But that fellow" wasn't a miner.
He was an Uitlander, you could tell
by the look of him, tallish, well set up,
carried himself even in that sort of safari suit
which didn't have much style to it. He was
different among others who were different,
he was looking at people differently
from others who saw others off.
Father fingered him with distaste.
"He was a German artillery officer."

Aunt Elsie

". . . could never make out why she did it.
Dammit, she was engaged to Gerry W——,
captain of the Kent team." You know the books,
the novels of his brother? And the other one's,
the Egyptologist, everyone knows them.
A damn fine family.
                    She broke it off.
Mother was very upset, as was Gerry's mother.
She married "That longnosedbastardthatsanctimoniousbrother-
in-lawofmine" (always run together).
"Kids in the East End called him Snorky.
He wanted to be a missionary.
The Bishop told Father that was the best thing."
He was sorry, but really, "We can't have the Church
made a mockery of in the streets, can we?"
Father agreed. The pity of it –
if not Gerry, then why not someone like
the parson's own brother, who took
the national four-forty championship
in a famous run: called to the starting line
he put down his pipe, ran his race, set
a record and was back before his pipe went out.
"Poor Elsie."
                She married. She left on her honeymoon
bound for the Sudan by way of Jerusalem
in a cholera year in the Holy Land.

Recruits 1899

Who hears a bout of bugles in an hour
which is the hour of need?
                              Why, such
young men as may be round about
and are put out to ride
and qualify.
                    All three asked
"What's your trade?" replied
"Sailor, sarmajor" so "Where
did you learn to sit a horse?"
answered

"Norwest Mounted Police
"BSAP Bechuanaland Border Patrol
"Egypt, with the Bimbashi

                              That was how"
they went about joining up, like
Seamen Three, what men be ye?
They answered
                    correspondingly.

Horsetrading: Stallions

The Tigers were Uitlanders and colonials. Judged as scouts and fighting men,
they were the elite of the army. . . . They looted as quietly and thoroughly as
they fought and scouted. – Thomas Pakenham

1

He had a Basuto pony.
"That pony could turn on a sixpence, you could shoot
from his back, he didn't mind, he wasn't
gunshy at all. If you had to go sniping
he'd just stand. Cunning, too:
when the column outspanned the bullocks were
turned loose. They'd be bound to hunt for the grain
wagons, try to stick a horn into a sack.
He'd follow them. If the grain started to run
he was on the spot. He'd wait, whip round,
plant his hooves on the bullock's nose,
then fill his belly. He was all brain,
that little bloke."

Captain Ronald Brooke, seconded from Seventh Hussars,
kept after him to sell the pony. He wanted him
to breed from, for polo. Finally Father gave in,
for seventy-five pounds. Brooke shipped him
    Home.

How did you get him?

"Oh, I was over near the Calendon River.
I met a Basuto boy riding. I thought 'That's a nice
    little chap.' I gave the boy a kick in the arse
and sent him on his way. He was
probably spying."

2

He came
    into camp just before nightfall
on foot, his saddle and gear over his shoulder.
He'd walked home, he needed a remount.

In an Onehunga bar on a Saturday afternoon
with Bob Lowry: Bob looked around, said "Let's go
over in the corner and talk to that old bloke"
who didn't get the name right. "Smithson?
I've never met a Smithson before
except in South Africa. He was a guide and scout
attached to us. I was Captain Quartermaster
in the (something or other) Contingent,
in charge of remounts. I was outside camp
one evening when Smithson rode in. He rode
into a gully and tethered his horse,
shouldered his gear, dusted himself over
and walked up to camp. He came to see me
after mess. He wanted a remount,
his horse had been shot under him. I told him
to wait till morning, if he got up early,
if he walked a bit away from the camp
he'd probably find one in a donga."

"Well, I'm damned." Father's eyes ran. "I remember
that, come to think of it. His name was Captain . . .
Coates. Captain Coates, dammit, and still alive."

Captain Coates: "He was a splendid soldier.
He was a terrible thief."

3

He had a grey stallion
which would singlefoot for miles.
Just slack off the reins, sit back
like slumping in a rocking chair.
"You could take forty winks
unless/until someone took a potshot."

When they approached the farmhouse,
a three or four man patrol, fire was
opened on them which was stupid
with the kopje close behind.

                                    One in front
under a bit of cover, the others circling,
it didn't take long.
                            The burgher dead,
his wife – a real Tant' Sannie – with black
powdermarks all over her . . . they gutted
the house, burned it, took what they fancied.
Father took the unlikely looking grey
which turned out very well as things
turned out for the long hauls given
the Basuto pony for close work
(they were the breed of troops which had
a couple of boys and three or four
remounts as matter of course to back up)
until the grey was shot under him.
His leg was broken, the medicos
almost ruined his shooting hand. While
things mended
                        he rode as wagon master
in a column, but

4

                        it wasn't much fun
                        out of the saddle.
One arm, one leg, scarcely one ambition.

King Solomon's Mines

Up on the border/over the border
wherever the border was
                    with Strathcona's
Horse 'distinguished by their fine physique,
and by the lassoes, cowboy stirrups, and large
spurs of the North-Western plains'
                    Sam Steele their colonel,
who rode at Red River?
riding with Ivan Jarvis whose brother was
Inspector NWMP who took Soapy Smith
at – Dawson? Things get blurred,
near the borders anyway
                    of Portuguese East
and the railway to Delagoa Bay.
Oom Paul in flight down the line to Lourenço Marques:
           'The last of the old-world Puritans, he departed
           poring over his well-thumbed Bible, and proclaiming
           that the troubles of his country arose, not from
           his own narrow and corrupt administration, but from
           some departure on the part of his fellow-burghers
           from the stricter tenets of the dopper sect.'
Sundown was bleak,
                    over whatever border
Sam Steele and his boys rode into a valley
with tumbled stones which caught enough of sun
to throw it back. Shaped
                    stones, millstones, grind
ing stones, used to crush quartz.
Discarded, when too much coated. They didn't crush
enough. They couldn't do better, all
flopped to their bit of rock, the troopers
chiselled with bayonets. Jee-zuss! "King Solomon's mines!"
You mean: The boys in Strathcona's couldn't tell
real stuff from fool's gold?

           . . . I ask you.

He Travels Fastest Who Travels Alone

Scouting the veld Father saw a lone rider,
eased his Martini sporting rifle (preferred
to service issue) and circumspectly closed.
Boers, people thought, might be skulking around.
Yet, the way that fellow set his horse he shouldn't
    be a Boer, however cunning.
Closed in and found, General Sir Bindon Blood:
"Hah!" things being as they were, perhaps
apologetic, "I seem to have lost my staff."

Not the same as on the North West Frontier.
A sense of space, those skies – like running free,
confusing. With, of course, some frisson as well,
the Boers' latest capital taken 'with their State
papers and treasure',
                Schroeder captured,
Botha and Viljoen skipped over the line and off
to the south. Eleven hundred prisoners,
one pompom gun, a broken Krupp artillery piece,
remnants of that big naval gun they snatched
at Helvetia. Good hunting by and large.

Did Father by any chance know much about
the Barberton district?

How little did it need to end it all

Father hunting was outfoxed,
                         went to earth on a treeless
kopje, sent off a couple of rounds
for appearance' and oldtimes' sake,
surrendered to Manie Maritz' commando.
A hard man, Manie, a bad name.
Also, he'd just taken a bullet through the arm.
Father was sorry about that.

For oldtimes' sake, meetings in Jo'burg bars,
Manie didn't shoot him out of hand.
The commando rode towards Namaqua,
into Bushmanland. They were roughly speaking,
a lot of them, all boys together.
Things were mixed up in those parts
in desert country where
                         somewhere they took
his horse, his boots. They gave him a rifle,
a fistful of shells. They rode away:

he walked. Then he walked some more.
He shot goats. He ate goat. He made goatskin
boots. When he found wild honey, he ate wild honey.
When there was water he sometimes drank.
He reached a river which is or isn't the Zak.
At any drift, a few Boers . . .

Recovering

Bushmen carried him in, he had enteric.
"In the sick quarters in Calvinia
they used to open my eyes in the morning
to see if I was
                looking at anything."
Starr Jameson passed through the ward.
Father was BSAP Bechuanaland Border Patrol,
he was South African Light Horse, Rimington's
Tigers, all boys together, so
                   transferred
to Wynburg to convalesce. He mentioned
Groote Schuur too.
              Kipling was shacked up
in the estate house at Groote Schuur.
Cape Town thought him a strange fellow, he sat
in trams with kaffirs. He eulogised Joubert
who 'gave his life To a lost cause,
and knew the gift was vain.'

Requiem

Rhodes died an inarticulate man,
like a boy in the little he could handle
words. Out of the blue Rhodes asked Kipling,
"What's your dream?"

Father was finished with having fevers.
Because he was there, a Company man, a soldier,
one of those young men who knew their way about,
he was roped in to the escort.
Up to the Matopo Hills – he'd been there
before. All in all, it was impressive.
Hard not to feel, a part of history
transacted. In the hills are many paintings:
animals move stiffly, humans are a stage
beyond conventional. You may see
a long way on a good day.

That's where they sent Rhodes down.
'Dreamer devout' Kipling said, also 'great
Kings return to clay'.

After Vereeniging

After Vereeniging, anticlimax.
How to do with, how does a man cope with
roaring silence?
                    A quick trip Home:
"What are you going to do now, Willy?"
Commerce, perhaps, a turn more or less
at honest pennies but first another turn
as commentator – an amusement park,
an arcade? – for a diorama of the War,
then back to Cape Town
                          trying to set up
a stevedoring business (he said his clerk
was C. J. Dennis?) which didn't go.

He rented the Duke of Somerset's lodge
(watercoloured by Mortimer Menpes)
at something or other Bay outside town,
lots of pleasant hacking thereabouts.

Early morning, he was riding up and over
to one of those deepwater coves which nibble
at the Cape ways. He looked from cliff edge
into a gentle swell. In slack water
a cow whale lay more or less on her side,
her calf sucking.
                    When he told this
he gave the impression that somehow
("I mean, you knew you'd never see the like
again") this amounted to decision.

Palm Wine

Darkest Africa, the White Man's Grave
not needfully for people of experience
or Mary Kingsley in her impossible skirts.
Specifically, Old Calabar, as bosun of the beach
should have been a cushy number.
He was quickly undeceived,

then found no British ship would take him off.
Only a German tramp, wanting to replace
one of the black gang who died heat- and fever
struck. That's how Father learned
about the Kaiser's coolies at firsthand
and began hating Germans.
                              In South Africa
were Germans, they were only not likeable.
At the Cape he didn't wait for her to berth.
He dived overboard and swam ashore,
just to make sure.

Nothing Ventured Nothing Gained

For chaps of more mature years some
thing I never got the hang of,
it wasn't dwelt on,
                    a quick trip from Alex
or Port Said down towards the Yemen coast
running rifles. A Turkish gunboat put
paid to that. Father was not explicit:
    A cobber perhaps from South Africa
met with, putting together a crew
in a bit of private enterprise
(these days, you speculate, was he
an agent of the Arab Bureau?)
landed up in a Turkish prison,
Father on the Somali shore hiked
to Djibouti. A dubious consul shipped
    him DBS.

This Isn't Right

How did he come to be a radical,
a militant radical? Sticks belonged to
the Primrose League, others of the family
were

"I came back from a voyage. We were working ship.
One evening I was leaving the East India docks,
in the streets around were hungry
women and kids. The men couldn't get work.
Jardine Matheson brought in Chinese
coolies because they could work them for less.
I thought, 'This isn't right. This just
isn't right.'"

Nightingales

In Wellington he chummed up with a son and heir
of a coastal shipping/freighting company
who was in love with (oh, blueball smitten for)
a politician's daughter.
                              They would climb
Tinakori slope at evening, Father with bird whistle,
Jim with horny cornet. They blew into nights
fresh as anything coming up from the south,
the devastatingly pure south, 'Last Night
the Nightingale Called Me'.
                              I cannot be sure
anyone understands this, but I should like to.

   In Te Kopuru a C of E lady spiderweb lined
of more than mature years was courted. She gave
her hand to a suitor who carried her off
honeymooning as far as Tangiteroria.
She had a nephew getting into politics
who looked like doing all right; she too was
politic, returned from Tangi 'a married woman'
to several villagers' raw delight.
"Floss," they demanded outside the general store,
"Floss, did he make the nightingale sing?"
"What's a nightingale?" I asked Mum, "What does . . ."
who was hauling me away before
I ever
            did not understand. I'm not sure
that any better now I understand if at all
though I should like to.

or a cliff fall

from aloft at Port Chalmers,
working out on a yard
had a footrope snap under him,
bounced from one bit of rigging
to another like somehow tumbling
through a catscradle until dumped
on deck *bruised bruised bruised*
stunned. Surprised, but not by joy

in the Transvaal his horse shot under him,
left leg broken and right hand mucked up.
"When I'm gone, you look after my leg.
They set six gold pins around that break"
which didn't help

        all that much
on the Kaipara bars outward bound.
A deckload of timber smacked loose.
Father dived over along with the kauri.
A cross sea picked him *helpless in strife*
with waters I was whirled up and threw
him back, into the winches, broke
the same leg, same place.
The skipper decided they'd lose too much time if
      and anyway it would be tricky trying to put
        into Onehunga so Father and another bloke who'd
        been lumbered were strapped to the saloon table
all the way to Melbourne

meaning (in the long run) he didn't have a hope
in hell of the Army taking him to tackle
the Germans when that chance came (which he was
sure was coming) without a bit of fiddling.
None the less or wiser he got there.
'Each day brought on its common miracle.'

sailing out of Melbourne, bosun
on an Italian barque, the owner as skipper.
Said to be a count, said to be a navy man,
he didn't know a thing about sail.
The crew who came out from Genoa had quit;
he signed on whoever he could get.
The pay was good. Father decided
his broken leg was healed and threw his crutches
over the side.
                    The first mate, Mister Rock, so old
he couldn't see to take a noon sight.
The second mate shook. The skipper liked
to lie in a hammock with a boy to wind
the phonograph for him. "Hey, mister, set
some sails, come listen my records,
have glasses of wine." Winds themselves sang
gutty bel canto.
                    He set them north
about New Zealand: "Stay up warm, heh?
Stay warm, some day we turn down Chile."
Father went aloft.
                    A nice warm day but hazy.
From the masthead he could see better –
and hear, surf breaking on the Ninety Mile.
"We nearly did what the *Forest Hall* did,"
take the beach 'on a weather shore, in calm
weather, and in broad daylight'.
Not to worry. "You be mate, mister. Have
some wine. Listen this" maybe
young Stracciari as Conte di Luna,
Vivra! Contende il giubilo, the surf
a sturdy distancing bass.

Writing Letters

How did he
get on, so long away from Home? Did he
ever write?
"Mother knew pretty well
where I was, mostly. Or where I'd been.
If I ran out of money I'd cable home
for fifty quid so she knew I was alive,
wouldn't she, and whereabouts? Besides,
nearly every year I'd meet up somewhere
with Dick Ayres, and Dick wrote home
every Christmas. Mrs Ayres would always
pass on a message to Mother.

"One year," he turned thoughtful, "I missed
seeing Dick, but I met his sister Ruby.
She was on a cruise. I knew where Dick was
supposed to be, so that year she wrote.
It wasn't any trouble to her, writing letters.
That's how she made a living, writing"
(vaguely) "books." He never read any.
"They said she made a good thing out of it."

They were dangerous, they put themselves
in danger, like children wandered too far
to be called home because it's falling dark
. . .
Letters of his are in library archives,
about union matters, brotherhood of the working
class, One Big Union. If he felt inclined
he could "put pen to paper".

even the blustering surge forgot to rave

that blizzard-ridden winter. Everyone tried
to sit it out but, blast on blast,
Baltimore waterfront burned and froze
as it burned. He lost all he had
"except what I stood up in"
when taking cover in a saloon found
a grubstake,
                    Jake Kilrain, last of the bare
knuckle fighters, nothing less than
legend, larger than most
life. Father remembered seeing Jake Kilrain
at the National Sporting Club, London,
sponsored by the legal uncle whose name
I can't remember. It came in handy.

Father liked to fight, if not in the same class.

Fragment

When? For how long? He ran a cutter
on the Potomac or about the Tidewater
freighting vegetables for Washington:

"Up in those little places
they'd get a circuit preacher once in a while.
It was like Naktmaal on the back veldt –
if he couldn't preach for four or five hours
he was no good.
                    The women sewed, or fed babies.
The men got up, went out for a smoke,
passed a jug around, had a pee,
strolled back for more."
                    They were not
his sort of folk, but when, where
does this fit in?

Boston

Made one trip to the Banks
on a bluenose schooner, over
the side in a dory longlining
for cod. The hell with Captains
Courageous. Thank you, but no.

To Brazil, on a barquentine,
a sweet little thing, very trim,
a family ship. The owner skippered,
took his wife with him, very motherly –
like having singsongs (hymns, songs of praise)
at the piano in the cabin. She was short
on provisioning, a hungry ship.

They carried back coffee and nuts,
slumped in the doldrums.
Father as long as I remember did not
care for coffee. At Christmas,
pushed the nuts along the table.

Called to their Colours

Springtime a young man's fancy lightly
turns to thoughts of Spanish Main
(Cuba Yucatan Honduras Costa Rica . . .)
palmettos rustling thinly. Fruit bats squeaked
like shutters. Then, and always, clouds
of whining skeeters. He turned into
Admiral of the Nicaraguan Navy almost
overnight.
                    Until that time Nicaragua
(Or was it Honduras?) had no navy.
Instead, it had revolutions.
Shipping agent for the United Fruit Company
in a smitten port Father became
for a while the sort of revolutionary
which might be better for business.

The new President sent down a decree,
"Make a flotilla" from one bankrupt
(beached) steamer quietly rusting away,
some deckhands easily come by, a fever
riddled engineer who smelt of rum and pox
who sobered up enough to make her turn
over with the safety valve tied down.
A presidential party came to cruise.

Not only bands were brave that brassy day.
The medals, the top hats, sashes, leg o' mutton sleeves,
their parasols – any man's heart might be
misgiving at the final touch
                              a field gun
lashed on the fo'c's'le to bang out
a salute downharbour honouring the brave.
    The gun recoiling
tore stanchions loose, bucked back into
the forrard hold, and through.
The crew in kapok jackets took to the tide.
The presidentials and their ladies, maybe they
    walked home? It didn't matter much.

Next week a counter-revolution, and a boat.
Tallyman, tally me no more banana.
Fleetfoot Father left town for Florida.

Gulf

get away then,
                    Old Man, set sail from
that shorebound sargasso sea in central
America was the tidal/
                    tideless rising
fall they called *revolution*, take
your course northwards, you're not

cut out for Geoffrey Firmin any more
than Bruno Traven. The farce of history –
responsible, consequent – a stone
on which you scratch nothing but delible,

you scarper hotfoot on a slowboat
to Tampa, picking up a job on a cruise
about the local waterways making a pitch
to tourists cramming Ponce de Leon and the like,
they wanted to hear, but heard
"Willy? Willy! Is that you, Willy?"
from a travelling aunt. You can't go home
again? You do not need.

                    Travel broadens
those who mind. He passed to Mobile
but couldn't see the moon of Alabama
for mosquitoes, no one could endure
nonstop racketing buckets of a dredge
keeping hand to mouth,
                    to New Orleans.
"God, that was something to hear.
The black stevedore gangs on the levees
singing" but somehow
                    headed west
towards Galveston with a stallion
at so many bucks a stand, good service
guaranteed
                    where the trail
                         peters out

London, San Francisco

If they drank (as claimed) in
some taverns/bars along the waterfront
(naturally) what did they talk about?

Why, every/things and nothings/much.

The People of the Abyss, which is every/
where (but when?) and those who are
Sea Wolves, of and as matters of course
capitalists/victims.
                    They drank too much.

It's a communal failing.

Fish Flesh and Good Red Herring

The West Coast, delicately imprecise
for all that sometime thud of surf
mysteriously after the Japanese taste.
Rain forests, shingle and granite, a vague
which is not even middle distance
in and out of Seattle, Vancouver, Alaska anchorages.
Mostly, San Francisco, after the earth shook.

San Francisco rebuilding built towards One Big Union.
Along that coast trace more than one line of fault.
Men sang from Joe Hill's Little Red Songbook/s.
He became a Wobbly, a walking delegate in Frisco,
        then south again.

1912

Capitalists and victims of, say,
Whatever became of the Liberals while
Professor Mills wrangled with Scott Bennett,
the TLCs and the Red Feds, the SDP and NZLP
and the ULP and IWWs and anyone else wrangled for

there wasn't one big union let alone
one big anything else except Capital.

Father did not sail seven seas, he shipped
out of Wellington, on the coast,
over the Tasman, maybe a stint up as far as
Thursday Island or thataway, sometime
up the Sepik, but back to/out of Wellington
'widely known as an I.W.W. supporter'
within the Seamen's Union.

The strike is the weapon of the working class.
Tom Young became General Secretary of the Union.
With Waihi out on strike the seamen helped
while the Union itself was taking shape,
the Australian Federated Seamen's Union had
just taken shape, and
                    can you not understand
        that here is a foe at hand

you have not fought before. Not this way

as he helped, smuggling in funds
apart from those banks and Government could keep
track of, so next year
they couldn't tap the same sources
readily.
                    Even so,
when the time came more money came
but not (who could expect it?) enough.

71

Money went out as well
to help the fight in the common cause
in Australia, especially Broken Hill
and God knows, looking at it now, how
little how pitifully little

                       from how few
of them, how few there were,
faction-ridden too

the old bulls, Kneen in Auckland and Belcher
   in Dunedin,
the middling bull Tom Young moving from
   centre to left of the ring
and the young bulls, Father as Asst/Sec
   in Wellington and Bob Gordon Asst/Sec
   in Auckland
on the left and not making out.

Those (now often fragile) pieces of paper,
the records.
            Going through them
suddenly I remember Bob Gordon
as sometime in the Depression
Father would chat with when we were
going around the wharves, he was
        a Harbour Board gatekeeper,

a quietish (and like Tom Anderson, who took
over the Auckland office) rather "scholarly"
sort of man.
           What else I remember is
Father had known him in South Africa.

By the end of September 1912 the best
place for a crash course in militant unionism
was Mount Eden,
                              sixty-eight miners gaoled
lacking means to be bonded to keep the peace
which was the peace of Bill Massey, the peace
of Cullen the Police Commissioner and Herdman
the voice of Justice, who sent in
extra cops, scabs, bully boys and ex-cons,
arranged batons and pistols
(and silenced the Inspector at Thames, removed
the Superintendent at Auckland who maintained
nothing like show of force was needed).

£1600 needed, £1600 appeared from
the hand of Erny Davis. "Why did I do it?
Simple enough – they didn't have any money
in Waihi, did they? Someone had to do it."
That was in November.

                              When they were boys
Father sailed with the Davis brothers
crewing on *Viking*, always liked Erny
but seemed not to remember
what he did to help Waihi.

From the Club

and out of the Club
he swam with Malcolm Champion, with
young Freyberg? –

not competitively, he wasn't
in their class.
It came in handy when the Companies
brought their ships into port
but not alongside, mooring them
in the stream.

He swam out, he went up the
or near enough to be heard
to tell the
crew what was happening ashore
news of
the strike
that's what he said

Strike

Brought up on stories of, dusty
romance of, the Strike of '13
I trundle off to archives and read
telegrams, few letters, catching

little of passion, something of intrigue,
something of factional fighting
but more of not even so much bread
and butter day by day workings
as very dry bread indeed with
little butter to it, yet

nonetheless something too of stuff
of dreams exceeding material fact
(the Union was only so few hundred men)
and possibility, unRomantic
possibility.

                  When
the War came how little it registered
in those documents. And the Class War,
how (now) pitifully little.
Frail catchcries, for so short
a time.
                  Nonetheless
questions, like: actions at law
where the Union lawyer seems to have
    been Sir John Findlay
just out of politics where he was
Attorney General and Minister of Justice.

Father Wrote to Lyttelton

                    ours must be
an extra brand of scabs.
They seem to enjoy it.
The *Maunganui* got away with
a crew of scabs with spurs and baton –
but I don't think the spurs will help
much to fill the fires,
though the batons might come in handy
for breaking up the coal.

   The most peculiar facet of the scabs
working on the wharf is that they are
often having small strikes
among themselves for more pay and kicking
up rows because they don't get
                            enough overtime.

Massey's Cossacks

They came in from the farms.
They liked the batons which Government made
for them; some liked better the batons
they made themselves.
                              Closing on Lyttelton
they found the road carpeted with sizeable
furniture tacks. When they charged in Featherston Street
marbles, glass stoppers, steel bearings
went under them. "A pity about the horses,
not about the Specials."

        Tom Young told an outdoors meeting,
"If they try to hit you, you hit them back."
In court this became Inciting to Riot,
but that was three weeks later,
and another month before he was sentenced:
three months on The Terrace.
Father ran the office.

                      The Cossacks rode
home. They were not wiser, but they'd won.

My Old Man said follow the van don't
dillydally on the way off went the van
with the Old Man in it
                                    along Lambton Quay
after the specials jumped him and stole
the union office keys. They'd already had
a go at the office. This time
they beat up Father, turned over the office
again: the cupboard was bare,
the union records hidden, no cash
in the till, no money in the bank.

   Tom Young was going to be charged.
Father went to Tommy Wilford, then
a Liberal M.P. who appeared for Young
at his appeal but couldn't for him
at the first hearing. Wilford sent him on,
to Sir John Findlay, who demanded
"How much money does the union have?
. . . Then that's my fee." He took the lot.

He put it into his books, he wrote a cheque
for the same amount, he made another account:
"It is likely the Government will shortly move
to seize union funds. The union now has no funds.
You will see me when necessary."

Also he acted for free.

Doing Time

Police were not all hostile; they'd wanted/
    been refused their own union early in '13.
Mostly they didn't care for the Cossacks.

Warders were not all hostile. On The Terrace
they arranged it so Tom Young worked outside.
They went easy on supervising.
                        Father went
up and down from the office. They could sit
and get on with business peacefully.

Tom Young did his time, and Harry Holland
not for the first time; his game leg came
from Broken Hill gaol. Others passed
in and out. It wasn't fair,
warders curiously firm about being fair.

Take Pawelka. I've heard it said
warders thought Pawelka wasn't treated right,
they were senior men who fixed it for
    Pawelka's last escape,
                   set it up for him
to be not out of gaol but shipped out as well
all the way to British Columbia.

Tom Young

was lambasted by Harry Holland.
Holland was a Socialist, Young a meliorist.
He came round to seeing all were victims
of their class and system.
                        In prison
food was fit for animals, the bread made
'excellent cricketballs', the idea of people
washing hadn't reached authorities.
Prison officers might ask who was/what was free:
'single officers are even locked in cells
                        at night'.
Young shifted from Henry George to more
like Wobbly attitudes.

                        Marxists were
moving in, especially F. P. Walsh.
In '27 Walsh took over. He beat Young down:
"Young was stunting the growth and develop
                        ment of a virile working class."
Before long Walsh turned on the CP.

            Father distant from union affairs
still had faith in the Labour Party
of all our toil and skill and pride and hope.

Illicit Cargo

After the Strike
Father was blacklisted.
The shipping companies
wouldn't have him aboard
even as a passenger.

He was smuggled out
on a Union Company boat
to look for work in Fiji.

The Boss at Dreketi

Umpteen years in India, twenty-something of them
Warrant Officer First Class, Royal Engineers?

He could handle men, also Indians. He did not mean
to be offensive; Indians were different.
He would make distinctions, except at Lodge.

Different Indians were different in their ways,
this lot from that lot, they spoke different,

they thought – God knows what, what god,
they thought half the time. He was himself

another matter of godly difference, Anglo
Irish. He drank
                with a crate beside him at
his desk. When he emptied a bottle he yelled "Boy!"
The punkah boy opened the door, the bottle sailed
out. Only an old Roman priest, a Frenchman,
could outdrink him doing his rounds.

In his time he was a legend. Myths came after.
R. L. S. and Kipling never got near writing
about, let alone Louis Becke or Jimmy Cowan.

Society

   Fijians he respected while making
social (or class?) distinctions:
the most of them he did not regard as Children
   of Nature, perhaps more proprietorially.
The local *buli*, now, he emerged
from Father's stories as kin to
Bosmabo of the River;
                        the Fijian medical man,
trained at Suva, topped off at Sydney,
a cross between a medical orderly, witchdoctor,
con man, one who was smart and had to be
outsmarted;
            the *ratu*, nothing but respect
for him, he was church school and Sydney,
a right collegian along with right people.
And Oliver – Oliver was a class apart,
an outlaw.

            He did not see them (in retrospect)
as victims. To an extent exploited, yes, of course,
yet also exploiting if able, understandably.
Yet with reserve: I saw him once
meeting with one of the, if not himself, the
highest in the islanders' hierarchy
to whom he was firm, cool, and probably
            presumptuous.
His attitude said, "I haven't tuppence in my pocket,
neither am I of a usurping line"
which was how he thought of the Cacobaus,
caring as little for as he cared
for the main merchant princes of Suva.
            Contrariwise he much esteemed
old Captain Robbie of Levuka

                        and once,
outside Milne and Choyce's in Queen Street
as it was, stopped, removing his hat to
the Queen of Tonga, recalling to her
some distant (if at all) memories
complimentary to her father

            not altogether a child of his times.

Upriver

Upriver Father met Solomon Islanders.
People said they were better than Fijians at contract work.
Village people didn't like them, they were black fellows
also savages. You could believe almost anything
about them.
                    Two local girls went missing.
Tongues wagged, the timbercutters, they'd be the chaps.
They went, like a small patrol, Scott the policeman,
a couple of his constables, Father, and Oliver;
Father made sure Oliver went too.

Not that they had any trouble.
They agreed at the camp they'd seen two marys.
Yes, they came to the camp. No, they weren't.
So where did they go when they left?
This was thought a good joke, they were a jolly crowd.
You see, the girls hadn't left

                          they were nice plump girls.
They hadn't had any nice plump girls in a long time.
After, they ate them. Back home . . .

". . . which is where they'll have to go."
The Inspector was firm. "They may be damn fine workers,
they may be easy to get on with, but go they must."
The Boss agreed. Everyone agreed,
arrests, trials, business like that would be pointless.
Father Petitjean doing his rounds gave his opinion,
they were probably Anglicans. They went home.
"They were damn fine workers."

The local chief offered to take over the contract.
Thoughtfully, upped the price a bit.

Idyll

Out from Dreketi rivermouth before daybreak
in the cutter with Oliver, finest type
of Fijian a man could meet – Father had
nothing but praise for him, immensely strong
gentle, thoughtful, devoted to his tiny wife,
a Rotuman. Paroled (an unfortunate death
deemed murder, nothing vicious) in the boss's
charge, no better bloke
                              to fish with
on a so idyllic morning.

Almost flat calm, then very pleasant airs,
mists changing shape, fish biting just enough.
Somewhere armies made their moves,
ridiculous aircraft rose, to fall.
Mists parted only a little
and
                    Oliver staring nudged him
to wideawake. Like a fish boated Father took
to the bottomboards under dropped canvas.
Either side of the cutter big fellows
        Scharnhorst, Gneisenau, Nurnberg
    trailing, steamed gothically
towards Suva, breathing their own clouds.
Towards Easter Island's bleakly Prussian
officer faces, which disregarded them;
to Coronel, to the Falklands . . .
end of the Imperial East Asiatic Squadron.
Von Spee never knew
                          how Oliver and Father
crammed on sail, whistling winds hot headed
for Labasa and the Government telegraph's
damp ineffectual batteries.

Scratchmark

Scratchmark
above his left wrist, spiderweb
mooncurve not noticed until I was
thirteen, maybe fourteen.

   A badtempered coolie ran amuck,
beat up one of the head women in the lines,
then rushed off into the canefields.

"I had to go after him, he was dangerous.
He tried to jump me, came out swinging
a cane knife. The horse I used was a hard
mouthed brute, he needed a cavalry bridle
   and a curb.
I'd looped the reins round my wrist, that's what
saved me, the leather broke the blow.
But it was nasty."
                  The Boss was away, his Missus
bound up the arm. He rode across country
for the doctor and the police, swimming
the rivers. Bad luck all round,
the Boss not home, Oliver out in the bush
hunting beef, the workers upset
though the Missus was able to look after them.
The wound healed better than expected.

What happened to the coolie?
He looked at me over a gap not to cross,
cold, flat, "I shot him," a little surprised
anyone should be so naïve.

Testimonial

merely two strips of what was once
a letter

                  his to certify
            has been in my empl
            Overseer for the last
            to commend him to
            and application.

    Dreketi, Fiji
           20 January 1915

                  and the kind of curlicue
                  trailed across from what's
                  missing that's probably
                  part of
                          the signature

Looks as though
he was something
under a year
in Fiji. (He wasn't
attested for the Army
until February '16.)

Is this when he sailed
with Captain Ross to
the Solomons or was
over on the Queensland
coast?
      If he went back
to sea, he couldn't have
shipped out of New Zealand,
he was blacklisted.

Max

Cousinhood, supple web, subtle net
which could not obviously catch
or, if catching, hold. At least, on the Scottish
side, until you touched some strand of it.
Then learned, as of this book,
    Call the author P. Those who are Ps are cousins
to the Qs, the Qs are cousins to the S-Ms
who are cousins to the M-Ss,
M-Ss are cousins to the M-Hs, cousins to the H-Ms.
"The M-Hs are our cousins" in context, H-Js
who are in the J line as distinct from the M line,
with strands like J-W. Father spoke
liturgically, of marrying in as well as
marrying out over centuries. How did
he know this, who was so seldom home?
What it came down to was not a text,
                only a clipping from
an obituary column, "That was Max, he was"
an M-H, he did not marry, he had no issue,
he disappeared bombarded on the Salient.
Father spoke affectionately of Max.

For the Record

His number was 14524,
6th Haurakis, of 2nd Battalion,
Auckland Infantry Regiment.

Attested, Trentham, 9 February 1916.
Discharged, Wellington, 25 October 1917
he then being 37 4/12 years
which he wasn't.

He served at home   168 days.
He served abroad   1 year 92 days.

Off to the Trenches

A private medical certificate could get you
into the Army; someone understanding there
also helped. That's how
Father joined the infantry with a leg twice
broken and a bit of a limp. He didn't
do much marching until Picardy –
he had charge of the CO's horse.
At medical inspections he was missing,
caring for the horse, exercising the horse.
                        "Mind you,
it wasn't always easy barging across
No Man's Land hoppy-go-quick, especially
when there were trenches" or a touch of gout
come to that. "Probably no worse
        than it was for others."

Armentières

The town was not in one piece,
nor was it abandoned. One in six of the townspeople stayed.
Numbers of buildings were useful, and the blind
   factory (a billet by night) kept up production.
A brisk twenty minutes stepped from town were the trenches,
No Man's Land was a little further.
Not all men were used to working shifts, but that was
   the fashion of employment.

The public baths were celebrated.
Good arrangements for laundry were much appreciated,
   piece work on the part of the mademoiselles
who also maintained estaminets, coffee shops, pastry shops
   and purveyed other comforts in demand.
Another occupation was conveying intelligence
to the enemy.

After three months the Aucklanders, who were succeeded
   by 51 Highland Division, went off.
2 Auckland passed to Allery.

Allery

Twelve days working up at Allery.
Good feeding, good drinking, a good night's sleep.
The sun shone, trees were trees, fields were truly fields.
A most enjoyable stay.

On the move again.
Guns could be heard, flares seen.
Four days more, intensive battletraining, on again
through Amiens, through to

                        find their bivvies
tucked away behind the naval twelve-inchers,
marginal to battle, a comfortable stroll from Albert
where the Virgin angled over the road
and everyone waited for Her to topple.
Great business of traffic, purposeful.
To Mametz Wood, to the line.
             They were entering the Somme.

2 Auckland and 2 Otago led the way over.
The night was deadly cold, light rain or mist
swept around. Gunfire grew, and rumour.
Some of the rumour was true:
for the first time they were seeing tanks,
the secret weapon. But the secret spoiled.

The Somme wasn't anything new, oh dear No.
Three months already, another couple to go.
Haig was learning. The day after the Aucklands
        went over the top Haig shifted three of his five
        divisions of cavalry, to the reserve.
They wouldn't be needed immediately.

'The advance was marked by admirable
direction, pace and alignment.'
In thirty minutes they'd reached their goal,
Switch Trench. They overlooked Flers, they glimpsed
        Gueudecourt.
Northwest, a 'picturesque' ruined monastery.
Gentle slopes, with woods. The tanks were not
        a success.

Others went on. The Aucklands dug in
under heavy fire. They were relieved that night,
pulled back, with over 300 casualties, roughly
half their strength. This was to get worse.

Rain came again, suddenly mud was everywhere.
They were in and out of the front
until early October. Weathers turned worse.

The year failed into misery.
Wind, rain, sleet, weathers had no kind words
for anyone, then frost and snow.
Their awful world washed white – supposed
the worst winter in fifty years.
A *Country Life* picturesque. Even warring stilled
for the better part of three weeks.

2 Auckland billeted near Laventie,
in farms around La Gorgue
but went up the line for Christmas.
The enemy was only middling bothersome.
In snow-bound fields hares careered.
They made sporting targets.

January began to feel as though muscles were
flexed. A gut feeling:
they/we were probing, more probing into
February. Raiding parties grew,
to platoon size, to company strength.

In February Second Aucklands retired
to play a war game on a mock up ground:
six inch deep trenches, piddling drains, creeks.
Frost made ready to break, thaw began making sure
soils in front of the line would not
be helpful. Game was over.

Five hundred men went out across in that raid,
largest raid the Division ever mounted.
6 Hauraki and 16 Waikato companies were
the first wave.
                    Snow fell again.

Hill 63

Intervals of drizzling rain between
hail   sleet   snow   heavier rain
sleet   hail   snow before

Hill 63 which faced Messines.
Messines was always there, the village on the height.
Another battle was brewing up.
Trenching, cable laying, enemy harassing fire,
snow   hail   sleet   rain and
mud.   Before long

       another Spring.

Neuve Église

Neuve Église was a rear area.
In the first week of May the enemy attended
to Neuve Église, by night.

It was, it must have been, somewhere about this
time Father ended service in the field.

and BIG BANG

In the beginning was, or in the end /
interim was, Father's Big Bang or his Black Hole
he pitched into, and the hole closed
over. He was turning to descend
the dugout

               when the shell landed.

A fragment came so near it sliced his bayonet
at shoulder height. His right eardrum
shattered. Which of course he didn't
know at the time because he was getting
buried, the trench wall collapsing
into their stinking hermitage with him
under, seen to go, then gone.

They dug, hard enough at any time –
but in gasmasks? That clay which was not
even clay any more, some unjust soil chemical
charnel, and the wet which wasn't just
rain or seep or longsoaking piss
but compound of all along with
gas, which he was breathing.

They got him out.
They sent him down the line, they sent
him Home. Years after

               one of them offered him a souvenir,
a shell fragment inched out from
the trench wall thought to be the one cut
his bayonet. "No, really," he said, he couldn't
honestly say he wanted it.

Recovering

          labels tied to wrists,
jolted on stretchers. Walton-on-Thames
couldn't speak, couldn't hear. They were
finding out
                 which meant
iodine swabs rammed down his throat
("Like doctoring a sick horse the way
they went about it")
                but he didn't turn
out useful. Brockenhurst: convalesced.
                  His childhood
was not far away.

Excursion

            from Brockenhurst, for those
who were mobile, like walking wounded
to visit at Ruthin Castle along
the way. This would be good for colonials
making them see what they didn't belong to
although they however belonged in Flanders.
He chose not to go
                 wondering
what on earth had become of Daisy,
her husband Pless, her kids
who were undoubtedly German and certainly
of age for military service.

Trophies

one leg twice broken, sundry other
broken bones,
               one deaf ear, damaged
lungs, something twisted in his guts
after the dugout collapsed on him

some service ribbons/medals with or
without   clasps

                    an inflatable silk-skinned
pillow small enough to fold into
a pocket along with a khaki (small
print) New Testament (from a sister)
and a sort of do-it-yourself manual
How to be a Soldier
in case you hadn't picked up the knack
plus a diary with a pencil fitted
into the spine

                 some pieces of small change.
One brass, with a hole in the centre,
was inexplicably Chinese;
he couldn't remember why,
                   his luck piece?
He doubted.
             A crown and anchor (linen) board,
some dice

Uncle Basil

Cleanshaven (but, a small moustache) face
in now a slightly foxed portrait study
fixed into habit of command
not gainsaid by relaxed posing
or by his (rather dashing) norfolk jacket,
little checked cap, washleather gloves
casually handled.
        Whether he was older or
younger I don't know, only:
he didn't marry, his favourite breakfast was cold
roast beef with a half pint of beer – as boys at school
they had a half of ale after their cold plunge
winter or summer, to start the day –
and was Major in either the Honourable
Company or RHA. He was blown up
somewhere in France.

Father
didn't
talk much
about
the First
World War.

Windsurfers   board riders   wetsuit people
this being no day for smallboat handling

I stutter a beach most emphatically yours
under dirty weather's southwesterly dark-
ening past   stockbrokers' town-
houses   directors' holdings   Christmas-
tree enclaves and threesome

peasant-style black oystercatchers on now
expensive lava flows. It wasn't like this
when for a while he had a flat at hightide
level, just over there. That he should
have been sometime buried, sometime dug up,
made this possible?
                        Of course. That he would
have scorned the costly outcome? Of course.
Have envied   youngsters dancing
their Jacob's coat sails shrewd, Channel-
wise?
                        Of course, because
really that was what it was all about,
wasn't it, for the chance to?
For anybody who wanted to:

Aunt Agnes

It does not do to be frail.
When three left home one daughter had to stay
with widowed mother and bachelor brother
who was not strong. She looked after
the housekeeper and whoever else,
was pious, played the cello, lost her sight
(going blind runs in the family) and failed
to outlive what she probably did not think of
as the Great War.

Back

He went back to sea:
not sail, unless to darker Western islands?
Something cross-Tasman? I don't know.
Steam, yes, across the Pacific –

Tofua, Navua, certainly *Niagara.*
Apia came into it, and Vancouver,
shipping out of Auckland, after

more Union fighting with Government and more
in-fighting in the union.

Father's Opium War

Advice given me by my father
should I fetch up at Apia (I was on
Final Leave) but I can't remember exactly
where there should be
                    a big old (some
sort of) tree with a deepish knothole.
He was losing a race with cops or Customs:
"If you feel inside that hole you should find
a tin with, oh, about (at that time) six hundred
quids' worth of opium in it. It should be alright,
it was hermetically sealed. I never went
back to collect."
                    About that time he gave up
going to sea what with one thing and another.
Mother was shocked to hear: "Bill, you didn't!"
but he did.

        A fellow looks over his hibiscus
fence down a lane where cows are tethered.
Someone obscurely is scampering off into
the great world beyond; people are always finding
themselves on the dark edge of universe,
losing the race, losing out, whose sneakers
make commas all over in dust. They often leave
behind things which they mean to go back for.
Man at his fence, does he even try
to understand? Some hanker after dreams.

    Chinese, fond as they were of gambling,
were also victims of capitalist exploiting.

1 September 1921

Father married Mum.

Not Being Born on Malaita

　　　　　　　　Captain Ross met Father
in Queen Street – "The man himself, I want
you to go to Malaita and take over
my plantation," there and then, like that.
Malaita . . . sound of romance, distant surf,
windy in the rigging, such a paperback
scenario.
　　　　　　　Mind boggles at what lies beyond
civility, which is shallow: from beach
to store and compound, hutments, ordered
palms. Then, jungle. I see this only
when half-asleep
　　　　　　　　　the trading station
where I might have been born.
Mum jibbed at the very idea. That was
Ross of the *Ysabel*, you understand.

Along the Western Viaduct my Old Man
spotted her, showed the nasty scars
along her bulwarks, hatchets, or did they
call them tomahawks? "When they put a boat in
in those days they went in stern first,
no more than two men ashore at a time."
There were Winchesters. Malaita had
the worst reputation, the longest.
Just before the War a government report,
'Cannibalism has been stamped out';
after the War the first report,
'. . . has almost been stamped out.' This was
years after Captain Ross wanted me born there,
I was, I would be, no problem.
Father may have been disappointed.

Five years later the Kwaio massacred tax
　　　　　　collectors.
Captain Ross kept in well with the missions,
he was always good for a helping hand
with labour contracts, with concessions

for freight or passages, backhanders
for headmen. Copra prices rose and fell.
Ysabel ended up on the River.
The last I saw of Captain Ross, he stood
outside the Waverley, he praised God,
he offered tracts to those who passed him by.

Marking Time with Seth Thomas

Witching hours in an Old Men's Home slumped under
an extravagant belvedere, pensioners' dreams –
tightfisted, covetous, convivial –
tangled in murk. Moonwrack sleepers cried
tongues of men not angels fragmenting
Gaelic, Scowwegian, Finn, Russ or Serbocroat
along with heifer and morepork
when winds sat in their wrong quarter.
The Home shocked like a straining brig
wrestling the harbour bars.

Father snored off with his good ear down,
confident. It would pass. Between times
however dark, however stormbeaten the timbers,
regularly his eight day Seth Thomas
ship's clock rang the watches paced
between Chidley's *Lightning* and *Cutty Sark*,
Spurling's *Harbinger*, *Blackadder*, *Thermopylae*
along the hall and the diningroom walls.

Lodge

Not Solomon in his glory among lilies
as good value as Father togged out
for Lodge
              white tie and tails, compact
satchel for his coveted apron,
a Curwen book of shanties – he was shantymaster
at the farmers / smalltime merchants / some
this / some that singsong after
serious business. He sang (we thought) better
than John Goss and the Cathedral Male
Voice Quartet on HMV 78s, which collected.

   Lodge was where they rode a goat
(all kids knew that) in a hall at Aratapu
between arum clumps. They met, they did things,
they sang and had a party after.
In diesen heiligen Hallen, mysteries:
they met upon the Level and they parted on the Square
with handshakes and codes. A Mason could always
recognise a worshipful brother and would help,
so when lights went out a brother helped.
Father was supposed to know how
because of the gas plant at the Home;
he went to fix with a brother who had a torch,
the torch failed, worshipful brother spoke
into Father's bad ear who naturally didn't
hear him, perhaps saying, "For God's sake,
give me a light!" so another brother struck
a match.

             In the morning I was taken
to see him, shape of a secret society
masked in cotton wool and croton oil.
They said he was my father, I screamed
the place down (in fear? in fury?) not
for the first or last time, denied, denying.

Fortune Hunting

A season of tough sou'westers.
Father rode our chunky mare out to Glinks
to see how our bach was standing up.
He had the collie with him.
    While Father nudged the mare into a canter
along the water's edge the dog dragged
filthy stuff from the tide. It stank
higher than any windblown heaven.
Father took the reeking stuff and heaved it
    as the water pulled back.
He wiped his hands on Betty's coat.
All three of them would have made anyone
    throw up getting a whiff, you can hardly
imagine
            how they met the first bloke
back in the village, who breathed in and bellowed
"Christ, how big is it?" The next bloke ran
for his horse. Like the US Cavalry they went
thataway.
            This was soon after one of the locals
was paid five thousand for the ambergris
he found.
            They were out of luck.
That was the nearest Father got
to being a stinking capitalist.

Alec 1

For a while before the War Alec and Father
sailed out of Wellington, partners
in a ketch running around the Sounds.
They met up again on the River.

Alec came back from the War decorated
by three governments, for clearing minefields.
He bought a schooner-rigged auxiliary,
named her for his wife (she sailed with him)
and went into trans-Tasman business.
From time to time they loaded on the River.
Jolly reunions then, visiting the Home,
in the cabin as they lay (say) at Dargaville.

Alec was convinced: a man could make money.
Also, there would be another war.
Eventually he had three ships built for him,
small neat (fast if need be) lowslung freighters,
all (it was said) in consultation
with the Admiralty. When war began
they could be converted rapidly to Q ships,
that was the idea. He hadn't quite worked out
how he'd command all three at the same time.
Still, he didn't doubt.

Driving

Father, you and the four cycle motor were
not compatible. Things went better
when we had the gig,
                       the mare between the shafts,
those splendid sidelamps, a wetweather
carriage rug with rubber on one face,
fake leopard skin the other. Rimington's Tigers
rode again, our collie perched behind.
The whip cracked impressive – that was how
to cut a dash en route to Dargaville.

Luckily the gig was not sold off
when you bought the Rugby tourer with its Red
Seal engine and its mica curtains. Very trim,
that model
                but the gig did not see out
era of the Essex Super Six, saloon, shade of
electric blue, chammy leather yellow wooden-
spoke wheels. A phase of untimely
(only temporary) affluence; even so, we did
not always have a car.

                     When Father bought the Rugby
he could see if a man treated a vehicle
the way he handled a launch he wouldn't have
problems. He almost made it home that day.
Later, he took lessons. Still, in crisis
his horsemanship asserted itself.
We were all likely to be unseated
or without, getting the hang of it, taking
fences stiff-lipped as though stiff with pride.

Keeping in Touch

Whistlestop for river boats, hardly more;
business had mainly moved upstream.
The boardinghouse sectioned and barged away,
mills and the shipyard silenced, urgent then
to keep in touch. This was where
wireless came, to help us out from debate
about butterfat futures, static and all,
bringing more than the word of Major Douglas
or Krishnamurti. Mr Culford Bell
from Karangahape Road correctly spoke
district names in his news, nobody guessed
what places were meant, or meaning.
Children's Hour Aunts and Uncles hinted
where birthday presents for some lay hidden.
What, one asked, did Dunedin say, Sydney,
or (would you believe?) Los Angeles?

Our wireless was a Crosley (does that name
sound right?) with a speaker like two brown plates
pressed face to face, an oblong box
with dials, the batteries on a stand below.
Dempsey fought Tunney, we carried the fight
direct. We were in touch.

One night Father was at Lodge.
Before she gave in and went to bed Mum tuned
to Brisbane and picked up a programme
which hadn't been advertised, Melba's
very last Farewell. "When he came home I was
still standing at the set. I hadn't thought
to sit down. It was uncanny, so clear,
like being in the same room, her voice
the way it was all those years before."
They called her Mimi, *Addio* she sang over
skinny pine plantations, across gum fields
into a shining night which might have been
false dawn above the raupo, through the river
presence, *Addio*.

Kismet

"Arabs, you know, they call it Kismet."
Mum was sceptical. At times we went without.
After (say) an interesting discussion
at the Gentlemen's Club or the Northern Wairoa's
private bar (where the Kirikopuni Balloon Loop
was planned) he drove south intently thinking
things over, but too late spotted a calf
on the road. If Father saw a calf
the car veered into a ditch. True, there were
ditches, there were calves, he was quick to respond.
Also, something like Fate conspired;
this happened too at race meetings.
Who could doubt, as my mother did?

                    Still, to be vindicated:
We went, the three of us, to reclaim the Super Six
from the panelbeater near the gasworks.
Father driving out watchful stopped,
passing cattle were giving trouble.
A bullock backed from the mob, dung-spattered arse
growing bigger till *Smack!* it grounded on
the right mudguard.
                    "Now do you see, Nan?"
bitterly, "do you see now?" reversing
noisily into the workshop. Drunk or sober
Father could reverse. Gordon Coates could not.

How to Make

If you are Grandfather you buy a section
in or alongside Collins Street, then you sail
away, you are wrecked, you lose everything.
Don't go back to Australia.
                              If you are Father
following so to speak in your father's steps,
in this case, a BSA landgrant in Bulawayo.
Anyone can see it won't amount to . . .
you don't even bother to lose the papers,
you just don't bother. Property is not
theft, merely peculation.
                              After Grandmother dies
you put part of the legacy into a pub
being built on a useful site – it was
the first county town. The county town
has since twice changed places
yet, like everything else hereabouts,
this must have a future.
                              A promising site,
no competition. Your cobber the lawyer
who advised you and arranged things does
time (with time off) for embezzling.

Cabaret

Mother (it was said) could always cook.
Father didn't get on with the new
Hospital Board doctor. The bottom was going
to fall out of Wall Street, very time
to go it alone. We quit the Home.

A period of "looking around" for
an opportunity, God knows what but it called
up a handful of acres, cabbage trees, kahikatea,
two cows, pending decision
overlooked by the local cemetery
formerly a musket war fort with a mission
station below. A restaurant, that was what
the town needed, an eatinghouse by day
cloudy with steam, by night a pillar's
fiery coloured lights, three nights a week
cabaret: dinner, dance, sounds of music, sounds
of mirth appealing to a woebegone River,
its riverine folk.
                Soils waterlogged underfoot,
times turned colder, returned soldiers plodded
off farms up Strugglers Gully.

Our parrot poisoned himself; the collie, paralysed,
was put down. That town needed a cabaret
like it needed a hole in the head. I was sorry
leaving the little farm, I was getting
into Lawrence of Arabia, some old sheet
over shoulder, a towelling keffiya,
my playway shotguns, our cabbage palms.
The Jersey heifer didn't mind being
a racing camel with an awful bony backbone
but nonetheless she wouldn't race.

Her studbook name was Faith's Angel.
Ominous skies were not propitiated.

To Point Chevalier or Even Further

Off to seek our fortunes in the City,
Point Chevalier no less.
                                 Lions at night
coughed in the Zoo, and outlandish screamings.
Father slept badly.
                            From house to house,
rooms here, a whole bungalow there,
a threesome of country mice we huddled
towards a mercantile future,
                                 one no-hoper dairy,
something more like promise in another
which failed
               as matter of course
lacking a right touch with icecream cones.
What could be sold off was sold.
Grandmother's rubies and garnets went

but our portable Brunswick gramophone
stayed on, lugged ineffably from point
to Point, dependably grinding
                           John Goss's
shanties, tearoom melodies, musical
comedy, Peter Dawson *The Floral Dance*,
Dussolina Giannini *Un bel di*.

Cheque to Your King's Children

Once there was a cheque particularly.
                    Father presented it at
the Bank of New Zealand, Queen Street;
Historic Places has an interest.
The sun shone
                    warmly on every facade.
Inside was some delay, a teller.
The Head Teller summoned, peered at, smiled
oddly, took the cheque away.
Others were called from duties, looked at,
dispersed. It was hoped we did not mind
waiting a minute or two. Father anxious,
halfway blustery wanting to assure
it was the family bank was assured nothing
was wrong, sir, nothing at all.
        "This cheque, you see, sir, is drawn
on Child's Bank. These young persons,
they've never seen a cheque from Child's Bank.
I thought, if you didn't mind, they should.
They may not see another."
        I had to pull my socks up and look lively.
Things were falling apart.

My Old Man on relief work helped build
Chamberlain Park which was then
the Stone Jug, after
         the Old Stone Jug
                              a square lava block building
where for years a family made the best of all
cough lozenges. Earlier it was a pub,
first of all a military blockhouse,
                    so they tore it down,
that bit of Old Auckland, and used the blocks
for the base of the clubhouse. They were
people who said a lot about men on relief
         (Starkie was in the same gang)
whose chests/legs/moving parts weren't so good
(nor clean bright and lightly oiled)
after the War, who fetched up close to notable
inventions only as wheelbarrow, as sled (pulled by
several hands), pickaxe, crowbar, seven pound hammer
or fourteen, with the privilege of fastening
themselves to a roller to flatten out
from scoria and lava fairway and putting green.

Regardless

      He told them
he didn't want their pension.
In the Depression he did want it,
they said he wasn't eligible. "Christ
Almighty, I had a pension offered me.
I turned it down because I didn't think
I'd need it. Now I need it."
         Letters were
written, clerks talked to, concluding
"Nothing ever happened to you."
They told him, Look at your discharge,
on account of pre-enlistment disability
aggravated by active service.

Hospital records? What was he treated for?
They didn't know, they didn't want to know.
There weren't any papers. He didn't believe
them, he tried
      tracking down nurses,
sisters, a matron, found the medical officer
in charge a something wrapped in a tartan rug,
"You mustn't tire him," who thought he could
remember the hospital, nothing more.

Eventually a clerk who'd been a digger told him,
"You may as well give up. We're not allowed
to say so, they had a fire in Wellington,
some files were destroyed. That's why
some men have no records." They just had
to soldier on regardless.

Adaptable

On one of our moves we rented a bedsit
with verandah and use of, from a Devonshire
couple. Our landlord didn't have to worry,
he was a skilled tradesman still in demand,
he specialised in tombstones.
  He was otherwise adaptable.

The wife's brother went down with *Victoria*.
In the diningroom a picture of his ship
which he had worked in wool.
                              The son of the house,
surly in his teens, went off to sea;
later, served in the Long Range Desert Group.

We thought of ourselves as adaptable people.

Work for Idle Hands

Grafton Gully is concrete spillway.
Our city's early dead huddled there not
disturbed by, methos and some on the vag
slept out/slept rough, stashed bedrolls
under the bridge, it hasn't gone
out of fashion.
                                    The unemployed cut paths,
the unemployed trimmed urban wildness.
Some jumped over. Some were lovers
who darkly gave thanks. They made
light work for the war wearied walking
wounded, with an agreeable foreman.

The Domain too they chipped, clipped,
cut back, shaped into semblance of control
halfheartedly. Out of season
Cenotaph wreaths wilted, they withered.
Loquats fruited, ducks on the pond by the kiosk
had to be grateful, for what was offered?
Father was seconded to the Winter Gardens.
He attended to dahlias, chrysanths, cyclamen
which had never heard of
    places with names on walls of the Museum.

Untitled

The Charitable Aid Board gave out
vouchers for groceries. Father's bad leg
wasn't good in queues, Mum went.

On Thursday late afternoons
at the side door of the Mill in Fort Street
for sixpence you could fill a kit
with broken biscuits. That was the best day,
they made chocolate biscuits
on Thursdays. I went,

also Saturday mornings, the local
R.S.A. put up parcels of meat
in a garage behind a house in Formby Road.
At their parties Mister Burgess
the milkman dressed as a schoolboy
with a cap that said Eaton College, said

come young blood
leave your prattle can you not
understand that here is a foe at
hand you have not fought before

Christmas one year, they gave me
a useful knife which any boy might need
who hadn't a horse to shift stones out
of the hoof of but next year
an automatic cap pistol. I slept
on, under my pillow.

Sail

Grace Harwar, *Passat*, *Pamir*:
"I want you to see this. You'll probably never
again" – he was right, never again – "see
three ships like these in port together."
Pamir was no thing of beauty, *Passat* neither.
Grace Harwar had more line, more style;
Father was between regard and scorn,
"My God, look at her gear. It's shoddy stuff."
Still, you wouldn't see the like again.

Magdalen Vinnen was another, a German, sort.
A smart ship, lines, sheets, brass, woodwork,
holystoned deck breathed true Nordic
(soon to be Aryan) style. Later
stubby *Joseph Conrad* and Villiers.
Father drank his tot but couldn't stand
an overplus of bullshit, would rather

look around or chat a while aboard *Huia*
that lovely creature, birthed at Aratapu,
late in her day sold to the French
(we knew no good would come of that) and broken
on a reef off New Caledonia.

                 Once
to the far side of the Western Viaduct
to look over a little thing, *Huon Belle*,
shaped along the Huon River in Tasmania.
She was the oldest vessel on Lloyd's Register,
one hundred and twenty something years
in service. Her ribs had adze marks on them,
touched instinct of them still viable,
scars of her convict builders.

Diversifying

The man next door had more than one section.
Mostly he grew strawberries. Also he saw
a future in rice. This was planted right up
to the footpath, it was handy to the tramlines
convenient (we said) for loading. He thought
a lot about the future.
                          For the present,
this way, that way, he got by keeping
open mind and options. Like the Fun Doctor
he was known all over, he pedalled here,
peddled there, carrying his gear
to school fairs, sports days, bring and buys,
church bazaars. Even, the Winter Show.
At that time nobody else knew how
to whip up candyfloss.

Henderson

                                    wasn't much fun.
A tightmouthed widower with a little kid
wanted a housekeeper. Mum filled the bill.
Father chipped weeds for the town board
relief scheme and helped make another
playing field.
                         You could take only
so much tucked away behind a wind
whistling engineering shop
where the man of the place (never any
doubt about that) was into wireless:
broadcast, the world spoke to him
from Los Angeles, Sydney, then in
short waves until he slept,

a Saturday night special under his pillow,
bedded down in a nowhere place.

Indians

Indians . . . they weren't Indians,
they were Hindus otherwise coolies
    often (downtrodden) victims, of
capitalist/imperialist oppression
particularly on the part of the CSR.
    I do not remember that
they were suffering masses,
he was not altogether sentimental.

    * * *

Indians rode around on shaky carts
(not as good to their horses as Chinks)
crying in thin high Hindu voices *I buy
bottle n bag*. They might be
persistent at the back door: "Laydee, are you
sure you haven't bottle r bag?"
    You put down your newspaper, you leaned
(perhaps) into sight, saying –
This was followed by a hawker touching
his forehead, crying "Sahib!" like
something in Kipling, and scuttling
    off.

    * * *

Indians kept shops.
Father did not like to be kept
waiting especially if he was passed by
for somebody better dressed. He might
lightly tap the floor with his stick
looking out into the street making
some remark, he did not raise his voice.
He looked over the road, for instance,
to the Astor where he might be going
to spend threepence after spending
threepence at the greengrocer's.

131

He said something. He was heard.
He would not have to wait again.

The main trouble was, really, just
that they didn't have any sense of ever being
part of One Big Union.

Boston Road

Visible prison was over the road.
Lots of ways a man can do a long stretch:
some quarried, some crushed stones, some
outside walls chipped weeds then went
inside again to end their days.

Father did most of the cooking.
He cooked on a kerosene heater
in our living room; he could make a rabbit
stretch three meals. Mum brought home bits
the blind might not see their way to eating.

Trusties were sent up Symonds Street
to do messages. Father shopped there or along
in K Road which nobody called K Road then.
I got on with my homework sucking
compulsive sweet juices from awful teeth.
"His teeth are rotting away in his head,"
people said, but Mum said to wait, best
make a clean sweep in one go.

Near the front door a framed photo
blown up big, a West Australian two year old,
our landlord's favourite action shot
of all he had taken when he was young,
one day at a bush track. Nobody saw
through dust and glare a rail sprung loose
from fitting a curve, the free end sharp.
The two year old pushing it ran right on
and right through, was standing there after
without a jock, not
something you see every day, is it?
Men stood around looking as though they might
go back chipping weeds any time now,
indeed yes, any time now. No doubt
they reckoned to make as clean a sweep
as they could in one go, and wouldn't forget.

Harry Holland

O not in sorrow shall ye walk
In slow procession to my tomb
But proudly march as though you come
To hail me victor in the fight –
When I am dead.

Joe Savage, Pat Fraser, Bob Semple, Bill Jordan, Nash,
    Parry, Langstone, Armstrong and all and all
F. P. Walsh, Arthur Cook, Angus McLagan and Big
    Jim Roberts and all and all and all

were walking and hailing
socialisation of the means of production, distribution
    and exchange of
The System
               not altogether in sorrow

Election Night

Election Night, whatever happened downtown
I was at the State in Symonds Street,
a nonstop marathon filmshow
until results were in, Labour was in,
to totter back bug-eyed
to our two rooms in Boston Road.
At thirteen was I yet a member of the Party?
I did duty, like the gods' messenger to Father
who wasn't much on going to movies.
    Mother was on duty at the Blind Institute.

The State set up a screen beside the screen.
On the left Hollywood's promising tall tales,
on the right results flashed 'as they came
to hand'. That was the first time I saw
a short (in Vistavision?), The Three Stooges.

* * *

The Three Stooges continued
producing shorts or something like features.
Their names were
                    anybody could see
really they were only imitation Marx
        bros.

A promised land, land of friendly roads.
The roads went onwards, and upwards in spite
of that old Adam who jammed signals, in
spite of Tooley Street, Montagu Norman, the Reserve
Bank's governor, all the conspirators.
After Henderson, Liverpool Street; after
Liverpool Street, Green Lane; Boston Road.
We were back to the Point again,
we had a house, we had our own Reserve.
Instead of renting rooms we rented.

A new deal for the man in the street.
Campaigning, for social justice.
Mum took to charring for ladies less able.
Father, coughing still, spat a little blood,
had gout less often, then not at all.
Wounds still ached.
                              All over front rooms,
diningrooms, kitchens showed
the face of Micky Savage. Radios spoke
him into family. Not ours, Father did not
call him Micky, referring to him as Joe.
Not because we were in Jack Lee's electorate,
more like because he wasn't Harry Holland.

Things a young person should know
to the tune of *Shenandoah* and *Shallow Brown*:
how to deal with
                    the case for Guild Socialism
                    the need for the Pacific
         Maritime Union
                    Communists (never trust, since
         the Second International)
                              never can tell, they might
come in handy
some day

                         I turned fifteen. He took me
to the Grey Lynn library, local
Labour Party branch meeting,
enrolled me.
                    The membership card said
about socialisation of means of
production, distribution, exchange.
Not for long.

Looking Backwards

The first Labour Government was in office.
A *fait accompli*, without consulting us
Mother went into time payment, again we had
a radio. We were in touch,
                            broadcasts from the House,
Eb and Zeb, Fred and Maggie, Father's good ear pressed
to the Speaker (this was better than Hansard)
and Gordon Hutter. Sense of purpose –
everything being built all over,
they hadn't yet started quite to fall apart?
On the horizon a shimmering like pearl.

Au fond du temple saint:
soon I was getting into opera, would rather
had been girls but girls were difficult.
Even so after Evensong I ratted on Maury,
left him with both choirgirls on his hands,
scuttling home to hear the latest tenor,
Jussi Björling.
                    Mother closed her eyes, Father leaned
against *E lucevan le stelle*, to *La donna è mobile*.
How right. "As good as Caruso, or better,
when I heard him in Philadelphia."
"Like Melba," Mum declared, "you don't know
whether to laugh or cry." We'd missed
Uncle Scrim.

                    Along skies westward stars were
shining, a flickering like not so distant gunfire.

Jack Lee Now

          he was something else,
man of letters as well as wingy
veteran, had fire in him, drew fire.
Where a question of credit, had credit,
wanted more, moving
                    into open warfare,
confrontation. A troubled term.

I voted for the expulsion of Jack Lee
eventually, from the Branch, along with
Wingy Douglas. For reason of
party solidarity? Or, because Lee moved
against those who were at some time in the fight,
men of the labour movement who became
the Labour Party? Union men, mainly.
Somewhere, something, went, wrong.

    Father's heart went out of politics.
Politics took to wearing dark homburg hats.
They made much of F. P. Walsh. The unions, too.
Compromise, the politic art.
                    Father was
disillusioned. You could have too much
compromised. When
               as the War ended Labour
got in, in Britain, where was the highly
romanticised face of the cardcarrying
worker?
           Under another hat, same style.

Inscrutable Chinese

Chinese
    were either profoundly a threat
to working class solidarity or
      they were
amiable if peculiar chaps always named John
which was convenient. They were very good
with collars.
    Father stuck with
detachable collars which when out of use
coiled in a circular cane box.
Even during the Depression Mother was
n't good enough at collars.
      Where collars
were starched were pakapoo tickets,
these could be usefully marked on
Fridays,
    and sometime paid off.

Chinese smoked opium in dens.
Dens looked like old shops on Hobson Street
or Grey's Avenue. Only older Chinese smoked,
they played fantan too. Nobody did
anybody any harm; everybody knew that,
except Chinese who were Presbyterians
and some of the cops who were Irish
and puritanically Catholic.

Telling Stories

Every so often son rebelled against father,
trying to catch him out, carping or sceptical.
Every so often was the doubter mocked:
        you met someone who not called to bear witness
        did so. "Bill, you remember – ?" and there
        it was
confirming South Africa, the Strike, something
on the coast.
                As he got older he might muddle
something he'd read with what he'd done.
He could be challenged then, but then
every so often was the doubter mocked.

        Struck once, impatient, over-confident.
A book of yarns about the sea, by Shalimar?
One tale in that already known; if not quite same,
then same enough. "I thought you told me
this, or something pretty like it
happened to you" accusingly.
                        He looked over
his glasses mildly. "I sailed with him
when he was going second mate. He used to write
        down things people told him.
He didn't get that story right, you know."

Veterans of the Foreign Wars

Edward, met at the Workingmen's Club,
discovered he and Father were in some nth degree
of cousinhood. This took several years.

Edward had forsworn his rightful name.
He chose to be called Hope. Kinship was
on Grandmother's (the Scottish) side. Still, helped
explain how they found themselves congenial.
Cousins, they were cousins everywhere, like
seeking like. They shared

                          ineffectual ambition,
feckless memories. Projected partnerships in,
inevitably came to nothing yet warmed moments
between halfhandles of draught Speights.
At time Edward and Father joined
in charitable work for the RSA,
attending funerals. Father held his hat
to his heart, Edward clutched a largish plump
     paper bag.
This caused lots of comment, you may imagine:
Enter Edward, with paper bag. He places bag
     on chair, carefully sits himself on it.

                    * * *   * * *

Remarks were made, little direct enquiry.
You couldn't very well, people have their ways.

   This was Edward's benefit of service.
An incident in a trench, a quiet afternoon
too close to Fritz for comfort, who quietly
popped one over, a rifle grenade.
"I happened to look down. There's this damn thing
in the mud behind the Major. Nothing much

a man could do. I pushed him out of the way
and sat on top of it. I was decorated of course,
I've more holes in my arse than a pepperpot."

In those days in the Club the bar was rather dark.
Old soldiers fighting over wars could see well
enough the way things were going and would have
  another before long.

Getting Bearings

Often back from the Workingmen's Club
or the Naval and Family
Father sang *Sally Brown* – never the same
words twice – *Shallow Brown*, *Shenandoah* and *Tom's
gone to Hilo*, wholeheartedly mournful.
He would put his heart into them
    but
what shall we do with, what will the drunken sailor
do next? He will instruct his son
in useful arts
                 to shape a course for the Horn by
getting a fix on the Diego Ramirez rocks
    to approach and enter the Kaipara Harbour from
the south and west in heavy weather
    how to
                  must be written down in the back
    of Whitcombe and Tombs red school atlas.
Put your heart into it, boy, man and boy.

Sometimes he took off for a week or so
with Jack Sampson in Jack's yacht,
Father with his walking stick and gammy leg,
Jack with his headaches, that Turkish bullet
under his skull.
                Kawau maybe, round Waiheke,
the Barrier, more likely the Wade
where bad weather was bound to hold them up
for two or three days downriver from the pub
at Silverdale.

A Penny for Any Old Guy

Josie was Jack's eldest daughter. She wore boots
when nobody, but nobody, wore boots even if
this was during the Depression, I mean
where could they have come from so long after?
     Josie was stringy blonde, that washed out
leftover sort of blonde seen in rural Kent
or down the East End, a distant tribute
like a dim goodbye to Jutish incomers.
It takes a while to get over some attacks.
Jack was himself stringy and half-dark.

His head gave him trouble aching of something
leftover by cause of
               the day after the ceasefire
they went out to bring in a mob of Turks supposed
to have surrendered. The Turks opened fire.
Jack was left for dead, came close to being buried.
He was shorn of his strength. His pain remained.

When they were merry, that was near Lofty
when Lofty was living there and used to drink
Sunday mornings in his garage with Jumping Joe
Savoldi who went into the OSS and almost did
for his general defending him at Anzio.

* * *

A bloke in the bar at the Naval and Family
came up with a souvenir: "I never liked
to tell you I was one of the burying party.
We always checked over the bodies, I've kept
this ever since . . ." and handed over
a twoheaded penny. Not everyone laughed.

145

* * *

One of Jack's sons was a guard at Featherston
when they opened fire on the Japanese prisoners.
Josie got married, went off somewhere,
I thought I saw her in London, Ontario,
turning a corner in a bigskirted coat,
fur hat, high boots, looking as though she'd done
alright for herself, but it can't have been.

How much depends, how you spin the penny?

Homing

Dougal sailed for Sanford's year after year.
He'd sit in the fo'c's'le with a plate of raw snapper,
getting on with his knitting waiting to bring the trawl in.
That was how they were, the Shetlanders or Orkneymen
and those like Dougal from the Hebrides.

Dougal was left some money. He set out off home.
At that time, to go home took six weeks at least.
He hardly seemed to have left, he was back again.
"Aren't you," Father asked, "supposed to be off
to Britain?" Dougal answered him, "I've been."

He left the ship at Plymouth, took a train,
another, through to Oban, the ferry for Stornoway.
At Stornoway he grabbed his bag, he lumbered
down the gangway and up the wharf. He looked
up the main street, he looked down, he said
"I do not like it." That was that,
back to the ferry, back to London, first
passage to Auckland.
                              Later I read poems
by expatriated Scots and realised I'd missed
the point (at the time) about Dougal's homing.

Jewel Song

           One Sunday night at Point,
Social Security debated, and Munich.
"When I was living in Sydney," Mum reminisced,
"I knew Melba's housekeeper. She called her
Boozy Nell. She took us backstage.
In the Jewel Scene Melba used her own.
A detective had to be there. Before he packed
away, he hung a necklace on me, pinned
other things – he said, Look now, you're wearing
fifty thousand pounds' worth. That wasn't much
before the War."
           Along western skies stars shone,
they flickered, like not so distant gunfire.

Pearl

Father was the sort of fellow who could
sit to a feed of greenlip mussels
to chip a tooth on
                                          a black seed pearl.
A mussel pearl it had to be, never
an oyster nor beyond price.
Still, he got a fiver for it
from Kohn's in Queen Street.

Horses for Courses

Take a list of acceptances, start reciting
the alphabet, when you get a starter whose name begins
    with the letter you've arrived at, that
    should be the one.
Or, close your eyes, stick a pin in the page.
Better still, follow a Chinaman to the tote,
    see what he backs and do the same.
Teacup readings? Not likely.
Inside information, then, straight from
the horse's mouth, but making allowance
    for what weight carried, likely state of track,
    breeding
            it might be as well only to go
for a place.

    Horses spoke to Father in confidence.
They weren't to be trusted. He used to laugh it off.
"It's all a gamble, isn't it?"
Some horses are mudlarks, some aren't.
A lot depends on the condition of the track,
much to be taken into account, thoughtfully.

A Regular at the Rising Sun

Father first met him in South Africa,
treating sick horses for the New Zealanders.
He had a way with him,
                              and later a dour plain
lumpy daughter who sat beside him in the pony cart
going to town delivering jars of ketchup,
relish, pickled onions, to their regulars.
He made a living otherwise treating sick horses
at the stables near the racecourse.

Then he had to go back to Yorkshire.
The brother he hadn't spoken/written to in thirty years
    was dead. Now the farm was his,
a lawyer wanted him for decisions on the spot
because the estate – my Old Man was staggered,
looking at the letter. "I said to him, Jesus,
Joe, you're rich. That's not a farm, it's an estate,
a real estate, and he said, Yes it was,"
when he was a boy, something to be proud of.
He wanted to farm it. His father wouldn't hear
any of that. "He wanted my brother there, not me."

"He made me go into medicine. I walked the wards
at Guys. The day I qualified I went home,
I gave him the parchment, I told him,
That's what you wanted, now you've got it
and bugger you, I'm off to the Cape"
sorry for sick animals, not people.

He went Home. He sold off everything.
He came back. The pony cart, the jars, just
like before, and the daughter too.

Fitting Out

Something paid off at the right time,
he needed a suit. He came home with two
from Victoria Street's bestknown outfitter –
unredeemed pledges. One a tropical kit,
fine picture of the planter on furlough;
the other a beautiful piece of cloth,
it needed a little work done on it.
A thing to marvel at in Boscawen Street
that cloth, the cut of it, no one for streets
around or up to the Hall stepped out
in a suit from Savile Row.
                              Father had
a friend to go with his Savile Row suit
whose Loewe pipes said to the world "Observe
what manner of man, what sense of proper values,
this." See them walking out, a suit, a pipe.

Devenish lived in the Queen's Head
on not much pension and occasional remittance.
A Captain, the Iniskillings, until axed;
a bit of land remained in Ireland;
his sister, the countess, looked after it,
widowed and quite as batty as any
in *The Irish R.M.* tales she slowly sold off
paddock and field, dealt him his share.

Father and Devenish strolled the town,
a turn round the wharves, a ride on the ferries.
Discussed, breeding of horses, affairs of state,
foibles of men. The expensive pipes,
they were a con job which began with one
found in a gutter, worked on, cracked with an axe
(the split suitably darkened), shipped off
to London *I thought you might like to see
this old friend . . . Palestine, Trucial States,
I could mention the North West* then wait
an answer: 'We have taken the liberty . . . displayed . . .
hope you will accept this cheque, these pipes . . .'

Should they
               for a change cross to Northcote?
The Empire was finished, and high time.
Soon the Germans would be at it again.
They might be needed.

Waverley

Captain Ross at the Customs Street doorway
handed out tracts, the Sallies peddled
their *War Cry*,
                    a sense of
the timeless as well as of the temporal
and of the timeless and temporal together
                    in one black-browed bar.
This, during one of those wars in the company
of men whose wars were not necessarily
same, who were not together in ships
at Mylae. Sighs shortly frequent were
exchanged
                    by Roy Lidgard, by a Vos,
by Billy Rodgers, by Shipbuilders' foreman
who hired old Charley Bailey after
his sons decided he was too old for work
and old Charley himself,
                    eighty past
on the way to ninety having trouble
hearing, presently halfcut, reminiscing
with my Old Man about taking a yacht
up to the King of Tonga, Salote's father,
with that Captain Piper who was thrown
out of the Union Company suspected
of running opium,

                    asked a question
dipped a finger in his beer and started
drawing on the bar, a twisted rheumaticky finger
which could explain better than words
line of a boat growing, corrected, flowing
to. Finger pointed up, amended logic
of a case, an aesthetic. Impressive, eh?
Then wiped out.

When I was kneehigh-to I might be walked
of a Sunday morning to the loft, its plans,
halfmodels, mockups, lines on a polished floor.

Mister Bailey with a cloth bent to wipe
clean, chalked in a new line freehand, swept
ribs and knees properly into place
timeless, and temporal, together.

    The Waverley's elderly barmaid (reputed
last of the old barmaids, serving out her time)
called "Time," cried "Gentlemen, please!"
O you who turn the wheel
                         and look to windward,
        look

Called to the Colours

"If I was of an age for this war that's coming
I'd try for the Air Force. That'll be the thing"
but when the war came once more he went
for a soldier.
           He didn't really expect
they'd take him for overseas, he was truly
hurt when they wouldn't take him at all,
furious
         when some pipsqueak ("I was soldiering
before that little squit was pupped, let
alone flying yellow at the mizzen")
halfheartedly suggested he could have a go
at Guards Vital Points however unlikely
they would have him.
                    He compromised,
on a Sunday morning caught a tram to Grey Lynn
joining the Home Guard. He was home for lunch.
"They tried to teach us how to fall in
and fall out, for an hour. Then,"
incredulous "they said they would show us
how to throw a hand grenade. Teach me
to throw a Mills bomb! They can get
stuffed." It wasn't right.

Alec 2

            The Navy wouldn't have him.
"Captain," they said, "you're doing fine,
go and help the war effort, sail your ship"
up and down, the Australian coast, the Tasman
crossings, the Islands, the war zone

terrifying his crew. He would go hunting
for Japanese submarines – they pleaded,
"Captain, sir, if we catch up with one
what will we do? We haven't any guns."
"We'll ram the bugger, that's what."
Suddenly Alec wasn't there anymore.

Someone at Admiralty remembered him,
winkled him out from the South Seas, thought him
not too old. He returned a while after
VE day. The British/Italian/Greek
          and Yugslav royals
decorated him for clearing the Adriatic mouth.
He came home in a yacht.
                  The yacht went aground
on an uncharted rock down the coast
in a part only recently surveyed again.
He was scathing in print about navy surveyors
who left unmarked rocks lying about.

Publishing

Father leaned and read. He didn't know
he was overheard. "In our family
we have had sailors, soldiers, lawyers and parsons.
We have never had a goddam poet,"
                    sighing heftily.

He went into the garden,
sat himself, arranging his game leg,
sowing peas. Whenever he sowed seeds like that
he whistled 'O promise me that someday
you'll be mine' between times swearing
at our black and tan bitch in Afrikaans
or maybe just a bit of Spanish.

He didn't guess he might be wrong,
on Grandmother's side a long time back,
could have been singing Hast thou seen
but a bright lily grow Before rude hands
have touch'd it? Have you marked the fall
of the snow or have
                    I got it wrong
stoutly bringing up the rear

The First Time and At Last

Mother said, "The first time
I saw him? He was a midshipman,
at Lyttelton.
                    He was a devil
for fighting."
Her folk never understood.

At eighty something: his doctor called
as I was passing the surgery,
"I've got your father's Xrays.
Look at this. I don't believe it,
his heart's only the size of a boy's."
We peered at shadows.
"And this – when did he have TB?"
I remember vaguely when TB was suspected,
but settled for a touch or two of gas
on the Somme.
                    Now he was slowly
going blind.

Cotton

At the end of our war I found
a copy of Charles Cotton's poems
sold off by Arthur Sewell. Arthur stopped
reading some day, marked his place
– 'Thyrsis, whilst our flocks did bite
   The smiling salads in our sight' –
with a handiest thing, a leaf.
                         It's still
         beautiful. Now an old gold, then
silver. My Old Man glancing
looked closer, took the leaf, turned it.
"That's from the silver tree. They grow all over
Table Mountain" and sat himself into
his fireside chair – the fire out, the chair
        stayed because of the dog and cat –
twisting the leaf against a distant light,
smiling, not saying anything more.

Books by Kendrick Smithyman still available from AUP

Stories About Wooden Keyboards, 1985, $16.95

Are You Going to the Pictures?, 1987, $22.95

Selected Poems, 1989, $22.50

Auto/Biographies, 1992, $19.95

Atua Wera, 2nd imp, 1998, $39.95